The
Chymical Wedding
of
Christian Rosenkreutz

The
Chymical Wedding
of
Christian Rosenkreutz

The Ezekiel Foxcroft translation
revised, and with two new essays

by
Michael Martin

⚜ Angelico Press

For information, address:
Angelico Press
169 Monitor St.
Brooklyn, NY 11222
info@angelicopress.com
www.angelicopress.com

978-1-62138-477-9 (pbk)
978-1-62138-478-6 (cloth)
978-1-62138-479-3 (ebook)

Cover art: "Allegory of The Chymical Wedding"
by Emi Shigeno
Cover design: Michael Schrauzer

For Bonnie

Arcana publicata vilescunt; & gratiam prophanata amittunt:
Ergo: ne Margaritas objice porcis, seu Asino substernere rosas.†

† "Mysteries made public are made vile, and thanks to profanation discarded: Therefore, throw not pearls before swine nor lay roses before an ass": the motto from the title page of the first edition of *Chymische Hochzeit Christiani Rosencreutz Anno 1459* (1616).

CONTENTS

FOREWORD

ENNYSON observed that most who sought the Holy Grail followed will-o-the-wisps into a marsh. In hardly any book is the reader at so great a risk of likewise losing the way and falling into reveries than in the enigmatic *Chymical Wedding*, perhaps, as its author would later say, intended more as a pastiche of alchemical allegory than as a straightforward esoteric text. The book becomes a magic mirror in which readers patently find their own spiritual concerns and ways reflected. What Michael Martin achieves in his version of Foxcroft's old and classic translation of the *Wedding* and in his commentary is to go through the mirror to what is surely the goal of all inner ways: the *mysterium coniunctionis*, the union of opposites, the inner unity we all seek and which, on the outer side, society today so urgently needs. Martin's work becomes, then, what the work in essence is: an invitation to that wedding of unification for which we were brought into being and which can and must be, as he wisely leaves in Foxcroft's drumbeat, received "This day, this day, this, this..."

BISHOP SERAPHIM JOSEPH SIGRIST

INTRODUCTION:
"So unlooked for an adventure"

HE *Chymische Hochzeit Christiani Rosencreutz anno 1459*, or *The Chymical Wedding of Christian Rosen-kreutz* as it is commonly rendered in English, is one of the most interesting texts of the seventeenth century, an era in which interesting texts fairly proliferated. It is also one of the most resilient and popular of the period and has provided scholars and speculators with multifarious opportunities for interpretation, most of which, indeed, are stranger than *The Chymical Wedding* itself.

Written, at least in draft form, by Lutheran pastor and theologian Johann Valentin von Andreae (1586–1654) during the first decade of the seventeenth century (probably in about 1605) while a student at the University of Tübingen, *The Chymical Wedding* did not see publication until 1616 and contributed to the "Rosicrucian furor" instigated by what have been called the two Rosicrucian "manifestos" (which, however, are not really of the nature of manifestos) the *Fama Fraternitatis RC* (1614) and *Confessio Fraternitatis* (1615)—which Andreae may also have had a hand in producing. Though, like the manifestos, published anonymously, Andreae later claimed paternity for *The Chymical Wedding* in his *Vita*, calling the work a *ludibrium*. "*Ludibrium*" is translated by some *CW* commentators as "joke" or "fantasy," which are serviceable choices, but perhaps a more accurate translation (and one closer to the spirit of the tale) is "game." *The Chymical Wedding*, like a perspective box, a *camera obscura*, or puzzle book is indeed like a game:

playful, inventive, insightful, offering delight alongside instruction. And, like all games, it is more fun when one plays along.

The story is full of jokes, puzzles, satires, and red herrings—mostly at the expense of academic pride and the pretensions of occultists. Adding to the humor of *The Chymical Wedding*, most of the commentary written over the last five hundred years in hopes of probing its secrets has been of exactly the sort Andreae was pranking in the first place—which is why he described the book's reception as "a game which was evaluated and foolishly explicated with subtle ingenuity and which proves the stupidity of the curious."[1] Indeed, some people don't know a good joke when it's played on them.

It is my contention that the playful construction of *The Chymical Wedding* is evidence of Andreae's intention to apply physic to the soul of the reader. The text, that is, serves as what Stanley Fish (one of the great readers of seventeenth-century literature before he turned to law and the life of a public intellectual) has called "a self-consuming artifact," which, as he further explains, "signifies most successfully when it fails, when it points *away* from itself to something its forms cannot capture. If this is not anti-art, it is surely anti-art-for-art's-sake because it is concerned less with the making of better poems than with the making of

---

1. "Superfuerunt e contra Nuptiae Chymicae, cum monstrorum foecundo foetu, quod mireris a nonnullis aestimatum et subtili indagine explicatum, plane futile et quod inanitatem curiosorum prodat." "Against these [lost works] *The Chymical Wedding*, which generated a brood of monsters, survived: a game which was evaluated and foolishly explicated with subtle ingenuity and which proves the stupidity of the curious." Johannis Valentini von Andreae, *Vita, ab ipso conscripta...* (Berolini, 1849), 10.

better persons."[2] As a self-consuming artifact, *The Chymical Wedding*—reveling in the high comedy of intellectual hubris, revealing its own "mysteries" despite its occult paraphernalia, and ever again reminding the reader to not rely on learning or the discovery of the secrets of nature as surrogates for salvation—tries to enact a transformation on the soul of the reader by destabilizing the reader's preconceptions of what a "chemical wedding" is—or, for that matter, what a "Rosicrucian" is. *The Chymical Wedding* succeeds when it fails (the sham "lost ending" certainly supports this supposition) because if it had succeeded as an occult text it would have surely failed as physic for the soul. Herein lies the brilliance of Andreae's *ludibrium*. That so many have missed what is so obvious only proves his point the more.

This willed ignorance, this intransigent and unrepentant misreading of a text, is something Umberto Eco in *Foucault's Pendulum* recognizes in some of the readers—certainly the enthusiastic among them—of allegedly occult texts. In Eco's tale three ragtag book publishers, in order to increase sales and revenues, decide to invent a secret society and its literature (as Andreae does in *The Chymical Wedding*)—which the world's occult "adepts" immediately accept as of authentic and esoteric pedigree. *Foucault's Pendulum* adopts all the epigraphical accoutrements of occult texts: quotes from the kabbalah (in Hebrew and untranslated), citations from the vast literature of esoteric adeptism, and so forth; but what this book really amounts to is a 560-page set-up of a joke. Once the publishing ruse is taken seriously by the adepts, things get seriously out of

2. Stanley E. Fish, *Self-Consuming Artifacts: The Experience of Seventeenth-Century Literature* (Berkeley: University of California Press, 1972), 4. Fish's emphasis.

hand—to the point where one of the publishers, Jacopo Belbo, finds himself on the verge of being made a human sacrifice at the hands of the occult brotherhood he and his associates invented and which the adepts assume they have been initiated into long since. At the point of execution, he utters the book's punchline: "*Ma gavte la nata*," a Piedmontese expression meaning "Take out the cork." As Eco's narrator explains earlier in the text, "You say it to one who is full of himself, the idea being that what causes him to swell and strut is the pressure of the cork in his behind. Remove it, and phsssssh, he returns to the human condition."[3] Now, in *The Chymical Wedding*, Andreae essentially tells the same joke: take out the cork. But, as with Andreae's, most occultists and conspiracy theorists didn't get Eco's joke either.

This is not to say that Andreae is wholly flippant when it comes to alchemical or other kinds of what we would now call esoteric ideas in *The Chymical Wedding*. As John Warwick Montgomery argues in his comprehensive (if slightly ham-fisted in its attempt to maintain Lutheran orthodoxy) scholarship on Andreae, the seventeenth-century theologian certainly found value in alchemy (he was from a family of practicing alchemists),[4] but to look for indications or insights regarding the secrets of alchemy in *The Chymical Wedding* proves a fruitless undertaking. First of all, Andreae follows neither the stages of the alchemical work found in Paracelsus or in Thomas Norton's *Ordinal of Alchemy*, nor in any other system. It may be that he had his own system

3. Umberto Eco, *Foucault's Pendulum*, trans. William Weaver (New York: Harcourt, 1988), 55.

4. See John Warwick Montgomery, *Cross and Crucible: Johann Valentin Andreae (1586–1654), Phoenix of the Theologians*, 2 Vols. (The Hague: Martinus Nijhoff, 1973), esp. 1: 241–55.

(which is Montgomery's guess),[5] but, more in keeping with his playful ethos throughout the text, it is likelier that the stages he represents in the text are purposely misleading, a way to play another practical joke on those looking for "the secret," another way to destabilize the reader's enthusiasms and expectations concerning allegedly occult "power."

So, given these characteristics, is *The Chymical Wedding of Christian Rosenkreutz* even worth reading in the twenty-first century? Most decidedly, it is. First of all, Andreae has provided us with a great story that Thomas Willard interprets as a Menippean satire,[6] or that, as Everett Bleiler and others have observed, is a kind of seventeenth-century harbinger of fantasy or science fiction—all genres as pleasurable as they are instructive about who we are as human beings.[7] Secondly, as an imaginative work and for what has been called "its irreducible strangeness,"[8] it is unequalled for playfulness and creativity, and functions in an apophatic space by refusing to be what the reader wants it to be (i.e., an esoteric mystery to be solved, or into which one might hope to be initiated). Finally, *The Chymical Wedding*, by refusing to lead readers into the experience they *desire*, nevertheless leads them into the experience they *need*, their very desire indicating a disorder of soul. *The Chymical Wedding of Christian Rosenkreutz*, then, is the esoteric text that is at

5. Ibid., 2: 278.

6. Thomas Willard, "Dreams and Symbols in *The Chemical Wedding*" in *Lux in Tenebris: The Visual and the Symbolic in Western Esotericism*, ed. Peter Forshaw (Leiden: Brill, 2016), 130–51.

7. See Everett F. Bleiler, "Johann Valentin Andreae, Fantasist and Utopist," *Science Fiction Studies* 35, no. 1 (2008): 1–30.

8. John Crowley, Introduction, *The Chemical Wedding by Christian Rosenkreutz: A Romance in Eight Days* (Easthampton, MA: Small Beer Press, 2016), 16.

one and the same time the antidote to esoteric texts: it provides the remedy by affecting the nature of the disease—the literary equivalent of Paracelsian medicine in which like is used to cure like.

About the Translation

Not much is known about Ezekiel Foxcroft (1633–1675), the first translator of *Chymische Hochzeit Christiani Rosencreutz* into English (as *The Hermetick Romance, or, The Chymical Wedding*, published in 1690) long after 1652, when Thomas Vaughan released his edition of the earlier Rosicrucian manifestos. Foxcroft was a scholar at Cambridge and close to the Hartlib Circle as well as to the Cambridge Platonists (Benjamin Whichcote was his uncle; Henry More and Ralph Cudworth were among his friends).[9] It has been suggested that Foxcroft knew Sir Isaac Newton and influenced the latter's interest in alchemy, which, while not proved, is certainly plausible if not universally accepted.[10] Whatever the case, he was without doubt a scholar interested in Rosicrucianism and its relationship to alchemy, or what has been called "the Counter-Enlightenment."[11]

Foxcroft's translation has been the basis for nearly every English version of *The Chymical Wedding* since, including

9. Richard S. Westfall, *Never at Rest: A Biography of Isaac Newton* (Cambridge: Cambridge University Press, 1983), 288.

10. Ibid. See also B. J. T. Dobbs, *The Foundations of Newton's Alchemy: The Hunting of the Green Lion* (Cambridge: Cambridge University Press, 1983), 112–15.

11. See John V. Fleming, *The Dark Side of Enlightenment: Wizards, Alchemists, and Spiritual Seekers in the Age of Reason* (New York: W. W. Norton & Company, 2013).

John Crowley's recent edition. In my treatment, I have not attempted to modernize the syntax or vocabulary. The quality of the initial cultural moment is too easily lost in trying to make classical or early modern texts "relevant" (as experiments with "making the Bible relevant to today's readers" have all too comically proved), and the resulting homogenization serves neither reader nor text. Nevertheless, I have tried to make the reading experience a little more palatable for the contemporary reader through providing paragraph breaks and punctuation according to contemporary norms and altering spelling judiciously and only for the sake of clarity. It has not been my wish to violate the text, but to make it and its period live for the reader in whatever small way I may be of service in that regard. Where this is not the case, the fault lies solely with me.

MICHAEL MARTIN
The Center for Sophiological Studies

HERMETICK
ROMANCE:
OR THE
CHYMICAL
VVEDDING·

Written in high Dutch By
Chriſtian Roſencreutz.

Tranſlated by *E. Foxcroft*, late Fellow of
Kings Colledge in *Cambridge*.

Licenſed, & Entred according to Order.

Printed, by *A. Sowle*, at the *Crooked-Billet* in *Hol-
loway-Lane Shoreditch*: And ſold at the *Three-Keys*
in *Nags-Head-Cenrt Grace-Church-ſtreet*, 1690.

Reader,

THe *Auther* was an extraordinary Perſon ; the Tranſlator a well qualified Judge; the Tranſlation is Curious ; And the Book Entertaining to any ſort of *Reader.*

Suſpenſa hedera nihil opus eſt.

L. F.

THE FIRST BOOK[†]

---

† There is no "second book" or third. This is one of Andreae's jokes, and, as we shall see, he makes many of them.

The First Day

N an Evening before Easter-Day,[1] I sat at a table and having (as my was my custom) in my humble prayer sufficiently conversed with my Creator and considered many great mysteries (whereof the Father of Lights[2] his Majesty had shown me not a few) and being now ready to prepare in my heart, together with my dear Paschal Lamb, a small unleavened, undefiled cake,[3] all on a sudden ariseth so horrible

---

1 As John Warwick Montgomery points out in his commentary, locating the *CW* here "sets the *Resurrection* tone of [the] entire book" (see his *Cross and Crucible: Johann Valentin Andreae (1586–1654) Phoenix of the Theologians: Volume II*, The Chymische Hochzeit *with Notes and Commentary* [The Hague: Martinus Nijhoff, 1973], 291). Some commentators assume this means that the first day takes place on Holy Saturday, though that is not at all clear from the text. Thomas Willard likes Palm Sunday as the starting point (which would make the sixth day fall on Good Friday— an auspicious day for alchemical death and resurrection). See his "Dreams and Symbols in *The Chemical Wedding*" in *Lux in Tenebris*, ed. Peter Forshaw (Leiden, NL: Brill, 2016), 130–51, at 141–42. Carlos Gilly points to an older tradition which places the opening of the *CW* on Holy Thursday in his edition of *Cimelia Rhodostaurotica: Die Rosenkreuzer im Spiegel der zwischen 1610 und 1660 entstanden Handschriften und Druke* (Amsterdam: In de Pelikan, 1995), 83. The important point, though, is that *any* date for the beginning of an alchemical work occurs prior to the resurrection.

2 James 1:17.

3 The Eucharist. The "Easter duty" of receiving the Eucharist on the feast is a feature in Catholicism and Eastern Orthodoxy, but not a strict obligation in Lutheran theology (Luther opposed the penal character of not receiving at Easter). See Martin Brecht, *Martin Luther: His Road to Reformation, 1483–1521*, trans. James L. Schaaf (Philadelphia: Fortress Press, 1985), 383.

a tempest that I imagined no other but that through its mighty force the hill whereon my little house was founded would fly into pieces. But in as much as this and the like from the Devil (who had done me many a spite) was no new thing to me, I took courage and persisted in my meditation till somebody (after an unusual manner) touched me on the back. At this I was so hugely terrified that I durst hardly look about me; yet I shewed myself as cheerful as (in the like occurrences) human frailty would permit. Now, the same thing still twitching me several times by the coat, I looked back: and behold it was a fair and glorious lady whose garments were all sky-colour and curiously (like Heaven) bespangled with golden stars. In her right hand she bare a trumpet of beaten gold whereon a name was engraven which I could well read but am as yet forbidden to reveal. In her left hand she had a great bundle of letters of all languages which she (as I afterwards understood) was to carry into all countries. She had also large and beautiful wings, full of eyes,[4] throughout, wherewith she could mount aloft and fly swifter than any eagle. I might perhaps have been able to take further notice of her, but, because she stayed so small a time with me and terror and amazement still possessed me, I was fain to be content. For, as soon as I turned about, she turned

4 "And their whole body, and their backs, and their hands, and their wings, and the wheels, were full of eyes round about, even the wheels that they four had" (Ezekiel 10:12). "And the four living creatures had each of them six wings; and round about and within they are full of eyes. And they rested not day and night, saying: Holy, holy, holy, Lord God Almighty, who was, and who is, and who is to come" (Rev 4:8).

her letters over and over and at length drew out a small one, which with great reverence she laid down upon the table and, without giving one word, departed from me. In her mounting upward, she gave so mighty a blast on her gallant trumpet that the entire hill echoed thereof, and for a full quarter of a hour after I could hardly hear my own words.

In so unlooked for an adventure I was at a loss, how either to advise or assist my poor self, and therefore fell upon my knees and besought my Creator to permit nothing contrary to my eternal happiness to befall me. At this, with fear and trembling,[5] I went to the letter, which was now so heavy as, had it been pure gold, it could hardly have been so weighty. As I was diligently viewing it, I found a little seal whereupon a curious cross with this inscription, *IN HOC SIGNO † VINCES*, was engraven.

As soon as I espied this sign I was the more comforted, as not being ignorant that such a seal was little acceptable, and much less useful, to the devil. At this I tenderly opened the letter and within it, in an azure field, in golden letters, found the following verses written:

> *This day, this day, this, this*
> *The Royal Wedding is.*
> *Art thou thereto by Birth inclin'd,*
> *And unto joy of God design'd,*
> *Then may'st thou to the Mountain tend,*
> *Whereon three stately Temples stand,*
> *And there see all from end to end.*

---

5 1 Corinthians 2:3.

THE CHYMICAL WEDDING

Keep watch, and ward,
Thy self-regard;
Unless with diligence thou bathe,
The Wedding can't thee harmless save:
He'll dammage have that here delays;
Let him beware, too light that weighs.[6]

Underneath stood *Sponsus* and *Sponsa.*[7]

As soon as I had read this letter, I was presently like to have fainted away, all my hair stood on end, and a cold sweat trickled down my whole body. Although I well perceived that this was the appointed wedding whereof seven years before I was acquainted in a bodily vision and which now so long time I had with great earnestness attended, and which by the account and calculation of the planets I had must diligently observed I found so

6 The symbol adorning the invitation is known as the *monas hieroglyphica* (hieroglyphic monad), introduced by John Dee in his (very baffling!) mystico-philosophico tract *Monas hieroglyphica* (Antwerp, 1564). Frances A. Yates makes a case for Dee as the inspirer of the Rosicrucian "movement" (if movement it can be called). See especially chapter III, "John Dee and the Rise of Christian Rosenkreutz" in her *The Rosicrucian Enlightenment* (Boulder, CO: Shambhala, 1978). Most scholars now suggest that Yates was overstating the case—and drawing some wild conclusions—concerning Dee's relationship to Rosicrucianism as it developed in the early 17th century. She certainly was. Nevertheless, the relationship of the monas to at least the invitation in *The Chymical Wedding* is hard to deny. See also the chapter entitled "John Dee: Religious Experience and the Technology of Idolatry" in my *Literature and the Encounter with God in Post-Reformation England* (Farnham, UK: Ashgate, 2014).

7 "Bridegroom" and "Bride."

to be, yet could I never fore-see that it must happen under so grievous and perilous conditions. For whereas I before imagined that to be a welcome and acceptable guest I needed only be ready to appear at the wedding, I was now directed to Divine Providence, of which until this time I was never certain. I also found by myself, the more I examined myself, that in my head there was nothing but gross misunderstanding, and blindness in mysterious things, so that I was not able to comprehend even those things which lay under my feet and which I daily conversed with—much less that I should be born to the searching out and understanding of the secrets of Nature, since in my opinion Nature might everywhere find a more virtuous disciple to whom to entrust her precious, though temporary and changeable, treasures. I found also that my bodily behavior, outward good conversation, and brotherly love toward my neighbour was not duly purged and cleansed. Moreover the tickling of the flesh manifested itself, whose affection was bent only to pomp and bravery and worldly pride, and not to the good of mankind. And I was always contriving how by this art I might in a short time abundantly increase my profit and advantage, rear up stately palaces, make myself an everlasting name in the world, and other the like carnal designs. But the obscure words concerning the three temples did particularly afflict me, which I was not able to make out by any after-speculation, and perhaps should not yet, had they not been wonderfully revealed to me. Thus, sticking betwixt hope and fear, examining myself again and again, and finding only my own frailty and impotency, not being in any wise able to succour myself and exceedingly amazed at the fore-mentioned threatening, at length I betook myself to my usual and most secure course.

After I had finished my earnest and most fervent prayer, I laid me down in my bed that perchance my good angel by the divine permission might appear and (as it had sometimes formerly happened) instruct me in this doubtful affair, which to the praise of God, my own good and my neighbours' faithful and hearty warning and amendment did now likewise fall out. For I was yet scarce fallen asleep when methought I, together with a numberless multitude of men, lay fettered with great chains in a dark dungeon: there, without the least glimpse of light, we swarmed like bees one over another, and thus rendered each other's affliction more grievous. But although neither I nor any of the rest could see one jot, yet I continually heard one heaving himself above the other when his chains or fetters were become ever so little lighter, though none of us had much reason to shove up the other, since we were all captive wretches. Now, as I with the rest had continued a good while in this affliction and each was still reproaching the other with his blindness and captivity, at length we heard many trumpets sounding together and kettle drums beating so artificially thereto that it even revived and rejoiced us in our calamity.

During this noise the cover of the dungeon was from above lifted up and a little light let down unto us. Then first might truly have been discerned the bustle we kept, for all went pesle-mesle, and he who perchance had too much heaved up himself was forced down again under the others' feet. In brief, each one strove to be upper-most. Neither did I myself linger, but with my weighty fetters slipped up from under the rest and then heaved myself upon a stone[8] which I laid hold of. Howbeit, I was several times caught at by others, from whom, as well as I might, with hands and feet I still guarded myself. For we imagined no other but that we should all be set at liberty, which yet fell out quite otherwise. For after the nobles, who looked upon us from above through the hole, had a while recreated themselves with this our struggling and lamenting, a certain hoary-headed ancient man called to us to be quiet, and having scarce obtained it, began (as I still remember) thus to say on:

> *If wretched mankind would forbear*
> *Themselves so to uphold,*
> *Then sure on them much good confer,*
> *My righteous mother would:*
> *But since the same will not ensue,*
> *They must in care and sorrow rue,*
> *And still in prison lie.*
> *Howbeit, my dear mother will*
> *Their follies over-see,*
> *Her choicest goods permitting still*

---

8 The notion of "the stone" is, of course, important in alchemy as the Philosopher's Stone, "a universal medicine because it can dispel all corruption, heal all disease and suffering, and bestow youth, longevity and wisdom" (Lyndy Abraham, *A Dictionary of Alchemical Imagery* [Cambridge: Cambridge University Press, 1998], 145). The Stone is likewise an analog of Christ. At this point in Christian Rosenkreutz's journey, the connotation bears just as heavily on scripture: "I love you, O Lord, my strength, O Lord, my rock, my fortress, my deliverer" (Psalm 18:2–3; 2 Samuel 22:2); "You form a building which rises on the foundation of the apostles and prophets, with Christ Jesus himself as the capstone" (Ephesians 2:20).

Too much in th' light to be.
Though very rarely it may seem
That they may still keep some esteem,
Which else would pass for forgery.
Wherefore in honour of the feast
  We this day solemnize,
That so her grace may be increased,
  A good deed she'll devise.
For now a Chord shall be let down,
And whose'er can hang thereon
  Shall freely be released.[9]

He had scare done speaking when an ancient matron commanded her servants to let down the chord seven times into the dungeon and draw up whosoever could hang upon it. Good God! that I could sufficiently describe the hurry and disquiet that then arose amongst us: for every one strove to get to the chord, and yet only hindered each other. After seven minutes a sign was given by a little bell, whereupon at the first pull the servants drew up four. At that time I could not come near the chord by much, having (as is aforementioned) to my huge misfortune betaken myself to a stone at the wall of the dungeon, and thereby was disabled to get to the chord which descended in the middle. The chord was

---

9 The gloss to both the German and Foxcroft first editions reads "*Vide S. Bernhard. Serm 3, de 7 fragmentis.*" As Montgomery notes, this is the only extra-biblical gloss in *CW*. It is odd, though, that Bernard's sermon is about God's infinite capacity for mercy, despite our many sins, while the *CW* speaks more to a meritocracy of election. See Bernardi, *Opera Genuina: Tomus Secundus* (Lugdini and Parisiis: Perisse Fratres, Bibliopolas, 1845), 322–24.

let down the second time, but many, because their chains were too heavy and their hands too tender, could not keep their hold on it, but with themselves beat down many another who perhaps might have held fast enough. Nay, many a one was forcibly *pulled* off by another who could not himself get at it, so mutually envious were we even in this our great misery. But they of all others most moved my compassion, whose weight was so heavy that they tore their very hands from their bodies and still could not get up.

Thus it came to pass that at these five times very few were drawn up. For as soon as the sign was given, the servants were so nimble at the draught that the most part tumbled one upon another and the chord, this time especially, was drawn up very empty. At this, the greatest part, and even I myself, despaired of redemption and called upon God that he would have pity on us and (if possible) deliver us out of this obscurity, who also then heard some of us. For when the chord came down the sixth time, some of them hung themselves fast upon it; and whilst in the drawing up, the chord swung from one side to the other, it (perhaps by the will of God) came to me, which I suddenly catching, got uppermost above all the rest, and so at length beyond hope came out. I exceedingly rejoiced at this, so that I perceived not the wound which in the drawing up I received on my head by a sharp stone before I with the rest who were released (as was always before done) was fain to help at the seventh and last pull: at which time, through straining, the blood ran down all over my clothes—which I for joy regarded not.

When the last draught whereon the most of all hung

was finished, the matron caused the chord to be laid away and willed her aged son (at which I much wondered) to declare her resolution to the rest of the prisoners. He, after he had a little bethought himself, spoke thus unto them:

Ye children dear
All present here,
What is but now complete and done,
Was long before resolved on:
What er'r my mother of great grace
To each on both sides here hath shown,
May never discontent misplace;
The joyful-time is drawing on,
When everyone shall equal be,
None wealthy, none in penury.
Who er'e receiveth great commands
Hath work enough to fill his hands.
Who er'r with much hath trusted been,
'Tis well if he may save his skin.
Wherefore your lamentations cease,
What is't to wait for some few days?

As soon as he had finished these words, the cover was again put to and locked down, and the trumpets and kettle drums began afresh. Yet could not the noise thereof be so loud, but that the bitter lamentation of the prisoners which arose in the dungeon was heard above all, which soon also caused my eyes to run over. Presently, the ancient matron together with her son sat down upon seats before prepared and commanded the redeemed should be told. As soon as she understood the number and had written it down in a gold-yellow tablet, she demanded everyone's name. These were also written down by a little page.

Having viewed us all one after another, she sighed and spoke to her son, so as I could well hear her, "Ah how heartily am I grieved for the poor men in the dungeon! I would to God I could release them all."

Her son replied: "It is, Mother, thus ordained of God, against whom we may not contend. In case we all of us were lords and possessed all the goods upon earth and were seated at table, who would there then be to be bring up the service?"

At this, his mother held her peace, but soon after she said, "Well, however, let these be freed from their fetters." This was presently done, and I, except a few, was the last. Yet could I not refrain, but (though I still looked upon the rest) bowed myself before the ancient matron and thanked God, who through her had graciously and fatherly vouchsafed to bring me out of such darkness into the light. After me the rest did likewise, to the satisfaction of the matron. Lastly, to everyone was given a piece of gold for a remembrance and to spend by the way: on the one side whereof was stamped the rising Sun, and on the other (as I remember) these three Letters, *D L S*.[10] With that, everyone had license to depart and was sent to his own business with this annexed intimation: *That we to the glory of God should benefit our neighbours, and reserve in silence that with which we had been entrusted.* This we also promised to do, and so de-

---

10 Traditionally interpreted as either *Deus Lux Solis* ("God, Light of the Sun") or *Deo Laus Semper* ("To God Eternal Praise"). In both the first German edition and Foxcroft.

parted one from another. But, in regard of the wounds which the fetters had caused me, I could not well go forward, but halted on both feet. The matron presently espying this, laughing at it, and calling me again to her said thus to me, "My son, let not this defect afflict thee, but call to mind thy infirmities and therewith thank God who hath permitted thee even in this world and in the state of thy imperfection to come into so high a light: and keep these wounds for my sake."

The trumpets then began again to sound, which so affrighted me that I awoke, and then first perceived that it was only a dream, which yet was so strongly impressed upon my imagination that I was still perpetually troubled about it and methought I was yet sensible of the wounds on my feet. Howbeit, by all these things I well understood that God had vouchsafed that I should be present at this mysterious and hidden wedding; wherefore with childlike confidence I returned thanks to his Divine Majesty and besought him that he would further preserve me in his fear, that he would daily fill my heart with wisdom and understanding and at length graciously (without my desert) conduct me to the desired end. Hereupon I prepared myself for the way, put on my white linen coat, girded my loins with a blood-red ribbon bound cross-ways over my shoulder. In my hat I stuck four red roses, that I might the sooner by this token be taken notice of amongst the throng. For food I took bread, salt, and water,[11] which by the counsel of an understanding person I had at certain times

11. For Paracelsus, these represented the essentials of life (Everett F. Bleiler, "Johann Valentin Andreae, Fantasist and Utopist," *Science Fiction*

used, not without profit, in the like occurrences. But before I parted from my cottage, I first in this my dress and wedding garment[12] fell down upon my knees and besought God that in case such a thing were he would vouchsafe me a good issue. Thereupon, in the presence of God I made a vow that if anything through his grace should be revealed unto me I would employ it neither to my own honour nor authority in the world but to the spreading of his Name and the service of my neighbour. With this vow and good hope I departed out of my cell with joy.

Studies 20 [2008]: 1–30, at 9). In alchemy, they correspond to sulphur, salt, and mercury; also, soul, body, and spirit. "Man consists of three things: sulphur, mercury, and sal. . . . Let that theory stand, then, that man consists of three bodies, and that one of these is salt, as the conservative element which prevents the body born with it from decaying. . . . Hence by parity of reasoning it is clear that man himself also must be nourished in some way: that is to say, that his Sulphur must receive nutrimental Sulphur, mercury its nutrimental mercury, and the congenital salt its nutrimental salt, whereby, from these three, man may be sustained and conserved in his species" (*The Hermetic and Alchemical Writings of Paracelsus the Great, Volume I: Hermetic Chemistry*, ed. Arthur Edward Waite [1894; reprt., London: Watkins], 257–58). As Montgomery (*Cross and Crucible*, 2:309) points out, they are also associated with pilgrimage. Note how later in *The Chymical Wedding*, when the homunculi of the King and Queen are created they are first described as being in the form of a "thin dough," which before the introduction of soul and spirit (blood and fire; sulphur and mercury) cannot yet be considered alive (131).

12 See Matthew 22:1–14, especially 11–14: "And the king went in to see the guests: and he saw there a man who had not on a wedding garment. And he saith to him: Friend, how camest thou in hither not having a wedding garment? But he was silent. Then the king said to the waiters: Bind his hands and feet, and cast him into the exterior darkness: there shall be weeping and gnashing of teeth. For many are called, but few are chosen."

The Second Day

I WAS hardly got out of my cell into a forest when methought that the whole heaven and all the elements had already trimmed themselves against this wedding. For even the birds, in my opinion, chanted more pleasantly than before, and the young fawns skipped so merrily that they rejoiced my old heart, and moved me to sing. Therefore, with a loud voice I thus began:

With mirth thou pretty bird rejoice,
  Thy Maker's praise enhanced.
Lift up thy shrill and pleasant voice,
  Thy God is high advanced.
Thy food before he did provide,
  And gives it in a fitting side,
        Therewith be thou sufficed.
Why should'st thou now unpleasant be,
        Thy wrath against God venting,
That he a little bird made thee,
        Thy silly head tormenting?
Because he made thee not a man,
O peace, he hath well thought thereon.
        Therewith be thou sufficed.
What is't I'd have, poor earthly worm,
By God (as 'twere) indicting,
That I should thus 'gainst heaven storm
        To force great arts by fighting?
God will be out-braved by none,

Who's good for naught may hence be gone,
O man b'herewith sufficed.
That he no Caesar hath thee fram'd,
To pine therefore 'tis needless
His Name perhaps thou hadst defam'd
Whereof he was not heedless.
Most clear and bright God's eyes do shine,
He pierces to thy heart within,
And cannot be deceived.

This sang I now from the bottom of my heart throughout the whole forest so that it resounded from all parts and the hills repeated my last words, until at length I espied a curious green heath whither I betook myself out of the forest. Upon this heath stood three lovely tall cedars, which by reason of their breadth afforded an excellent and desired shade and whereat I greatly rejoiced. For although I had not hitherto gone far, yet my earnest longing made me very faint, whereupon I hasted to the trees to rest a little under them. But as soon as I came somewhat nigher, I espied a tablet fastened to one of them, upon which (as afterwards I read) in curious letters the following words were written:

Hospes salve: si quid tibi forsitan de nuptiis Regis auditum,
Verba haec perpende. Quatuor viarum optionem per nos tibi
Sponsus offert, per quas omnes, modo non in devias dela-
baris, ad Regiam ejus aulam pervenire possis. Prima brevis
est, sed periculosa, et quae te in varios scopulos deducet,
exquibus vix te expedire licebit. Altera longior, quae cir-
cumducet te, non abducet, plana est et facilis, si te Magne-
tis auxilio neque ad dextrum, neque sinistrum abduci
patiaris. Tertia vere Regia est, quae per varias Regis nostri

delicias et spectacula viam tibi reddet jucundam. Sed quod vix millesimo hactenus obtigit. Per quartam nemini hominum licebit ad Regiam pervenire, utpote quae consumens et non nisi corporibus incorruptibilibus conveniens est. Elige nunc ex tribus quam velis, et in ea constans permane. Scito autem quamcunque ingressus fueris, ab immutabili fato tibi ita destinatum, nec nisi cum maximo vitae periculo regredi fas esse. Haec sunt quae te scivisse voluimus; sed heus cave ignores, quanto cum periculo te huic viae commiseris, nam si te vel minimi delicti contra Regis nostri leges nosti obnoxium, quaeso dum adhuc licet per eandem viam qua accessisti domum te confer quam citissime.

[Greetings, guest! If you may have heard of the wedding of the King, then attend to these words. Our Bridegroom avails to you through us four ways to the royal castle if you do not wander into byways:

The first is short but perilous and will lead you over rocky places from which you will be hardly able to escape.

The next is longer and will lead you in circles, not directly, but is flat and easy if you with the help of a compass are neither to the right nor the left led astray.

The third way truly is royal, which through a variety of delights and wonders you may undertake the journey. But hardly one man out of a thousand has been able to attain it.

Through the fourth no man may come to the kingdom, for it is a consuming path and not convenient except to incorruptible bodies.

Choose now which of the three you wish and on that constantly remain. But know that whichever path you will take was destined to you by Fate and that not without great peril will you be able to turn back.

These are the things we wish you to know. But beware, the ignorant, how much peril you undertake on this path: for if you have in the least way broken the laws of our King, I ask that you swiftly return home by the way you have come.]

Now as soon as I had read this writing, all my joy was near vanished again, and I, who before sang merrily, began now inwardly to lament. For although I saw all the three ways before me and understood that hence forward it was vouchsafed me to make choice of one of them; yet it troubled me that in case I went the stony and rocky way that I might get a miserable and deadly fall; or, taking the long one, I might wander out of it through by-ways, or be other ways detained in the great journey. Neither durst I hope that I amongst thousands should be the very he who should choose the Royal Way. I saw likewise the fourth before me, but it was so environed with fire and exhalations that I durst not (by much) draw near it.[1]

Therefore, I again and again considered whether I should return back or take any of the ways before me. I well weighed my own unworthiness, but the dream still comforted me that I was delivered out of the tower— and yet I durst not confidently rely upon a dream. I was so variously perplexed that, for very great weariness,

[1] Montgomery reads these four ways in two contexts: in a theological context connecting them with the Parable of the Sower (Matt 13; Mark 4; Luke 8); and in an alchemical context, associating them with the four elements: the rock-laden way with earth; the way of "Fire and Exhalations" with fire; the Royal way with air; and the "circuitous" way with water. See *Cross and Crucible*, 2:311.

hunger and thirst seized me and I presently drew out my bread and cut a slice of it. At once a snow-white dove of whom I was not aware sitting upon the tree espied the bread and therewith (perhaps according to her wonted manner) came down and betook herself very familiarly to me. I willingly gave my food to her, which she received, and so with her prettiness did again a little refresh me. But as soon as her enemy, a most black raven, perceived it, he straight darted himself down upon the dove, and taking no notice of me, would needs force away the dove's meat, who could not otherwise guard herself but by flight. And then they both together flew toward the south, at which I was so hugely incensed and grieved that, without thinking what I did, I made haste after the filthy raven, and so against my will ran into one of the aforementioned ways a whole field's length. And thus the raven being chased away and the dove delivered, I then first observed what I had inconsiderately done, and that I was already entered into a way, from which under peril of great punishment I durst not retire. And though I had still wherewith in some measure to comfort myself, yet that which was worst of all to me was that I had left my bag and bread at the tree and could never retrieve them. For as soon as I turned myself about, a contrary wind was so strong against me that it was ready to fell me. But, if I went forward on my way, I perceived no hindrance at all. By this I could easily conclude that it would cost me my life in case I should set myself against the wind. Therefore I patiently took up my cross,[2] got upon my feet, and

2 Matt 16:24.

resolved, since so it must be, I would use my utmost endeavour to get to my journey's end before night.

Now although many apparent byways shewed themselves, yet I still proceeded with my compass and would not budge one step from the meridian line.[3] The way was oftentimes so rugged and unpassable that I was in no little doubt of it. On this way I constantly thought upon the dove and raven, and yet could not search out the meaning, until at length upon a high hill afar off I espied a stately portal to which, not regarding how far it was distant both from me and the way I was in, I hasted because the sun had already hid himself under the hills. I (by far) could elsewhere espy no abiding place, and this verily I ascribe only to God, who might well have permitted me to go forward in this way and withheld my eyes that so I might have gazed beside this gate. To the gate (as was said) I now made mighty haste and reached it by so much daylight as to take a very competent view of it. Now it was an exceeding royal beautiful portal, whereon were carved a multitude of most noble figures and devices, every one of which (as I afterwards learned) had its peculiar signification. Above was fixed a pretty large tablet, with these words: *Procul hinc, procul ite profani,*[4] and other things more that I was earnestly forbidden to relate.

As soon as I was come under the portal, there straight

3 The importance of the Aristotelean Mean is not to be underestimated in early modern philosophy and natural science.

4 "Far hence, far the profane," a standard formula for mystery schools and cults. Montgomery ties this utterance to *Aeneid* 6.258, when Aeneas enters the underworld. See *Cross and Crucible*, 2:317.

stepped forth one in a sky-coloured habit, whom I in friendly manner saluted, which though he thankfully returned, yet he instantly demanded of me my letter of invitation. O how glad was I that I had then brought it with me! For how easily might I have forgotten it (as it also chanced to others) as he himself told me. I quickly presented it, wherewith he was not only satisfied, but (at which I much wondered) shewed me abundance of respect, saying, "Come in, my brother. An acceptable guest you are to me!" and withal entreated me not to withhold my name from him.

Having replied that I was a Brother of the Red-Rosie Cross, he both wondered and seemed to rejoice at it, and then proceeded thus, "My brother, have you nothing about you wherewith to purchase a token?" I answered my ability was small, but, if he saw anything about me he had a mind to, it was at his service. He having requested of me my bottle of water—which I granted—he gave me a golden token whereon stood no more but these two letters, S. C.,[5] entreating me that when it stood me in good stead, I would remember him. After this I asked him how many were got in before me, which he also told me, and lastly out of pure friendship gave me a sealed letter to the second porter.

Now, having lingered some time with him, the night grew on, whereupon a great beacon upon the gate was immediately fired that if any were still upon the way he might make haste thither. The way where it finished at the castle was on both sides enclosed with walls and

5 *Sanctitate Constantia* (Constance in Piety) or *Spes Charitas* (Hope and Love).

planted with all sorts of excellent fruit trees. On the side of every third tree lanterns were hung up, wherein all the candles were already lighted with a glorious torch by a beautiful Virgin habited in sky-colour—which was so noble and majestic a spectacle that I yet delayed some-what longer then was requisite. At length, after suffi-cient information, and an advantageous instruction, I friendly departed from the first porter. On the way, though I would gladly have known what was written in my letter, yet since I had no reason to mistrust the por-ter, I forbare my purpose and went on the way until I came likewise to the second gate, which, although it was very like the other, yet was it adorned with images and mystic significations. In the affixed tablet stood *Date & dabitur vobis.*[6] Under this gate lay a terrible grim lion chained, who as soon as he espied me arose and made at me with great roaring: whereupon the second porter, who lay upon a stone of marble, awaked and wished me not to be troubled or affrighted, and then drove back the lion. Having received the letter which I with trembling reached him, he read it, and with very great respect spake thus to me: "Now welcome in God's Name unto me the man whom of long time I would gladly have seen." Meanwhile, he also drew out a token and asked me whether I could purchase it? But I, having nothing else left but my salt, presented it to him, which he thankfully accepted. Upon this token again stood only two letters, namely, S. M.[7]

6 "Give and it will be given to you."

7 *Studio Merentis* (Merit in Study), *Sal Mineralis* (Mineral Salt), *Sal Menstrualis* (Menstrual Salt/Salt of Purification).

Being now just about to enter discourse with him, it began to ring in the castle, whereupon the porter counselled me to run apace, or else all the pains and labour I had hitherto taken would serve to no purpose, for the lights above began already to be extinguished. At once I dispatched with such haste that I heeded not the porter—in such anguish was I—and truly it was but necessary: for I could not run so fast but that the Virgin, after whom all the lights were put out, was at my heels, and I should never have found the way, had not she with her torch afforded me some light. I was, moreover, constrained to enter the very next to her—and the gate was so suddenly clapped to that a part of my coat was locked out, which I verily was forced to leave behind me: for neither I nor they who stood ready without and called at the gate could prevail with the porter to open it again, but he delivered the keys to the Virgin, who took them with her into the court.

In the meantime I again surveyed the gate, which now appeared so rich as the whole world could not equal it. Just by the door were two columns. On one of them stood a pleasant figure with this inscription: *Congratulor*.[8] The other, having its countenance veiled, was sad;[9] beneath was written, *Candoleo*.[10] In brief, the inscriptions and figures thereon were so dark and mysterious that the most dexterous man upon earth could

8 "Congratulations."

9 There is tremendous significance pertaining to the "veiled virgins" as compared to Venus unveiled on "The Fifth Day" of the narrative. The veil is the passageway to the mystery; it both covers and reveals. See note 2 to "The Fifth Day."

10 "Condolences."

not have expounded them. But all these (if God permit) I shall e'er long publish and explain.

Under this gate I was again to give my name, which was this last time written down in a little vellum book, and immediately with the rest dispatched to the Lord Bridegroom. Here it was where I first received the true guest token, which was somewhat less than the former, but yet much heavier. Upon this stood these letters: S. P. N.[11] Besides this, a new pair of shoes were given me, for the floor of the castle was laid with pure shining marble. My old shoes I was to give away to one of the poor (whom I would) who sat in throngs, howbeit in very good order, under the gate. I then bestowed them on an old man.

After this two pages with as many torches conducted me into a little room. There they willed me to sit down on a form, which I did; but they, sticking their torches in two holes made in the pavement, departed and left me thus sitting alone.

Soon after I heard a noise, but saw nothing, and it proved to be certain men who stumbled in upon me; but since I could see nothing, I was fain to suffer and attend what they would do with me. Presently perceiving them to be barbers, I entreated them not to jostle me so, for I was content to do whatever they desired. At this, they quickly let me go, and so one of them (whom I could not yet see) fine and gently cut away the hair round about from the crown of my head, but on my forehead, ears,

---

11 *Salus per Naturam* (Salvation through Nature) or *Sponsus Prae-sentandi Nuptiis* (Wedding Guest of the Bridegroom).

and eyes he permitted my ice-grey locks to hang.[12] In this first encounter (I must confess) I was ready to despair; for inasmuch as some of them shoved me so forcibly, and I could yet see nothing, I could think no other but that God for my curiosity had suffered me to miscarry. Now these invisible barbers carefully gathered up the hair which was cut off and carried it away with them.

Following this, the two pages entered again and heartily laughed at me for being so terrified. But they had scarce spoken a few words with me when again a little bell began to ring which (as the pages informed me) was to give notice for assembling. They then willed me to rise, and through many walks, doors, and winding-stairs lighted me into a spacious hall. In this room was a great multitude of guests—emperors, kings, princes, and lords, noble and ignoble, rich and poor, and all sorts of people—at which I hugely marveled and thought to myself, "Ah, how gross a fool hast thou been to engage upon this journey with so much bitterness and toil, when (behold) here are even those fellows whom thou well know'st, and yet hadst never any reason to esteem. They are now all here, and thou with all thy prayers and

---

12 In religious life, tonsuring is an important step in marking the movement from one state or role of life to another. It is part of the Order of Baptism no less than in the movement from vow to vow in religious orders. In alchemy, the symbol of shaving indicates a likewise preliminary stage in preparation for the realization of new, regenerated states of being. In the third-century Gnostic text *The Visions of Zosimos*, for example, the protagonist meets with a barber who initiates him into the secret of transformation. See C.G. Jung, *Alchemical Studies*, volume 23 in *The Collected Works* (Princeton: Bollingen, 1967), 57–108, at 60–61.

supplications art hardly got in at last." This and more the Devil at that time injected, whom I notwithstanding (as well as I could) directed to the issue. Meanwhile, one or other of my acquaintance here and there spake to me: "Oh, Brother Rosenkreutz! art thou here, too?" "Yea, my brethren," replied I, "the grace of God hath helped me in also." At this they raised a mighty laughter, looking upon it as ridiculous that there should be need of God in so slight an occasion.

Now, having demanded each of them concerning his way and found that most were forced to clamber over the rocks, certain trumpets (none of which we yet saw) began to sound to the table. There they all seated themselves, every one as he judged himself above the rest. As a result, for me and some other sorry fellows there was hardly a little nook left at the lowermost table. Presently the two pages entered, and one of them said grace in so handsome and excellent a manner as rejoiced the very heart in my body. Howbeit, certain great Sir Johns made but little reckoning of them, but fleired[13] and winked one at another, biting their lips within their hats and using more the like unseemly gestures. After this meat was brought in, and, although no one could be seen, yet everything was so orderly managed that it seemed to me as if every guest had had his proper attendant.

Now my artists,[14] having somewhat recruited themselves, and the wine having a little removed shame from their hearts, they presently began to vaunt and brag of

13 For "fleer": "A mocking look or speech; a sneer, a gibe; 'mockery expressed either in words or looks,'" *OED*.

14 That is, "alchemists."

their abilities. One would prove this, another that, and commonly the most sorry idiots made the loudest noise. Ah, when I call to mind what preternatural and impossible enterprises I then heard, I am still ready to vomit at it. In fine, they never kept in their order, but whenever one rascal here, another there, would insinuate himself in between the nobles. Then pretended they the finishing of such adventures as neither Sampson nor Hercules with all their strength could ever have achieved. This one would discharge Atlas of his burden, the other would again draw forth the three-headed Cerberus out of Hell. In brief, every man had his own prate, and yet the great lords were so simple that they believed their pretenses, and the rogues so audacious that, although one or other of them was here and there rapped over the fingers with a knife, yet they flinched not at it, but when anyone perchance had filched a gold chain, then would all hazard for the like. I saw one who heard the rustling of the heavens. The second could see Plato's Ideas. A third could number Democritus's atoms. There were also not a few pretenders to the perpetual motion. Many an one (in my opinion) had good understanding, but assumed too much to himself—to his own destruction. Lastly, there was one also who would needs out of hand persuade us that he saw the servitors who attended, and would still have pursued his contention had not one of those invisible waiters reached him so handsome a cuff upon his lying muzzle that not only he, but many who were by him, became as mute as mice. It best of all pleased me that all those of whom I had any esteem were very quiet in their business and made no loud cry of it, but acknowledged themselves to be misunderstanding men to whom the mysteries of Nature were too high and they themselves much too small.

In this tumult I had almost cursed the day wherein I came hither. I could not but with anguish behold that those lewd vain people were above at the board, but I in so sorry a place could not rest in quiet, but one of these rascals scornfully reproaching me for a motley fool. Now I thought not that there was yet one gate behind through which we must pass, but imagined I was during the whole wedding to continue in this scorn, contempt, and indignity, which yet I had at no time deserved, either of the Lord Bridegroom or the Bride. In my opinion, he should have done well to have sought out some other fool to his wedding than me. Behold, to such impatience doth the iniquity of this world reduce simple hearts. But this really was one part of my lameness, whereof (as is before mentioned) I dreamed.

And truly this clamour the longer it lasted, the more it increased. For there were already those who boasted of false and imaginary visions and would persuade us of palpably lying dreams. Now there sat by me a very fine quiet man, who oftentimes discoursed of excellent matters. At length he said, "Behold, my brother, if any one should now come who were willing to instruct these blockish people in the right way, would he be heard?"

"No, verily," replied I.

"The world," said he, "is now resolved (whatever comes on it) to be cheated, and cannot abide to give ear to those who intend its good. Seest thou also that same cockscomb with what whimsical figures and foolish conceits he allures others to him? There one makes mouths at the people with unheard of mysterious words. Yet believe me in this: the time is now coming when those shameful vizards[15] shall be plucked off and all the world shall know what vagabond imposters were concealed behind them. Then perhaps that will be valued which at present is not esteemed."

Whilst he was thus speaking (and the longer the clamor lasted, the worse it was), all on a sudden there began in the hall such excellent and stately music as all the days of my life I never heard the like. Immediately, everyone held his peace and attended what would become of it. Now there were in this music all sorts of stringed instruments imaginable, which sounded together in such harmony that I forgot myself and sat so unmovably that those who sat by me were amazed at me. This lasted near half an hour, wherein none of us spake one word; for as soon as ever anyone was about to open his mouth, he got an unexpected blow. Neither knew he from whence it came. Methought since we were not permitted to see the musicians, I should have been glad to view only all the instruments they made use of. After half an hour this music ceased unexpectedly, and we could neither see nor hear anything further.

Presently after, before the door of the hall began a great noise sounding and beating of trumpets, shawms, and kettle drums, also master-like, as if the Emperor of Rome had been entering. Thereupon the door opened of itself, and then the noise of the trumpets was so loud that we were hardly able to endure it. Meanwhile, (to my thinking) many thousand small tapers came into the

15 Masks.

hall, all which of themselves marched in so very exact an order as altogether amazed us. At last the two afore-mentioned pages with bright torches entered the hall, lighting in a most beautiful Virgin, drawn upon a glori-ously gilded triumphant self-moving throne. It seemed to me she was the very same who before on the way kin-dled and put out the lights, and that these her atten-dants were the very same whom she formerly placed at the trees. She was not now as before in sky-colour, but arrayed in a snow-white glittering robe which sparkled of pure gold and cast such a lustre that we durst not steadily behold it. Both the pages were after the same manner habited (albeit somewhat more slightly).

As soon as they were come into the middle of the hall and were descended from the throne, all the small tapers made obeisance before her. Then we all stood up from our benches, yet every one staid in his own place. Now she having to us, and we again to her, shewed all respect and reverence, in a most pleasant tone she began thus to speak:

The King my Lord most gracious,
Who now's not very far from us,
As also his most lovely Bride,
To him in troth and honour ti'd;
Already, with great joy indu'd,
Have your arrival hither view'd:
And do to everyone and all
Promise their grace in special;
And from their very hearts desire
You may it at the time acquire;

That so their future nuptial joy
May mixed be with none's annoy.

Hereupon with all her small tapers she again courteously bowed, and presently after began thus:

In th' invitation writ, you know
That no man called was hereto
Who of God's rarest gifts good store
Had not received long before,
Adorned with all requisites,
As in such cases it befits;
How though they cannot well conceit
That any man's so desperate,
Under conditions so hard
Here to intrude without regard;
Unless he have been first of all
Prepared for this nuptial.
And, therefore, in good hopes do dwell
That with all you it will be well:
Yet men are grown so bold and rude,
Not weighing their ineptitude,
As still to thrust themselves in place
Whereto none of them called was:
No cockscomb here himself may sell,
No rascal in with others steal;
For they resolve without all let
A wedding pure to celebrate.
So then the artists for to weigh
Scales shall be fixed th'ensuing day;
Whereby each one may lightly find
What he hath left at home behind.
If here be any of that rout

Who have good cause themselves to doubt,
Let him pack quickly hence aside;
For that in case he longer bide,
Of grace forelor'n and quite undone
Betimes he must the gantlet run:
If any now his conscience gall,
He shall tonight be left in th' hall
And be again released by morn,
Yet so he hither ne'er return.
If any man have confidence,
He with his waiter may go hence,
Who shall him to his chamber light
Where he may rest in peace tonight;
And there with praise await the scale
Or else his sleep may chance to fail.
The others here may take it well,
For who aims 'bove what's possible,
'Twere better much he hence had passed,
But of you all we'll hope the best.

As soon as she had done speaking this, she again made reverence and sprung cheerfully into her throne. Thereupon the trumpets began again to sound, which yet was not of force to take from many their grievous sighs. So they again conducted her invisibly away, but the most part of the small tapers remained in the room; and one of them accompanied each of us.

In such perturbation 'tis not well possible to express what pensive thoughts and gestures were amongst us. Yet the most part resolved to await the scale, and in case things sorted not well, to depart (as they hoped) in peace. I had soon cast up my reckoning, and, being my

conscience convinced me of all ignorance and unworthiness, I purposed to stay with the rest in the hall,
choosing much rather to content myself with the meal I
had already taken than to run the risk of a future
repulse.

After that, everyone by his small taper had severally
been conducted into a chamber (each as I since understood into a peculiar one). There stayed nine of us, and
amongst the rest he also who discoursed with me before
at the table. But although our small tapers left us not,
yet soon after within an hour's time one of the aforementioned pages came in, bringing a great bundle of
chords with him. He first demanded of us whether we
had concluded to stay there, which when we had with
sighs affirmed, he bound each of us in a several place,
and so went away with our small tapers, leaving us poor
wretches in darkness.

Then first began some to perceive the imminent danger, and I myself could not refrain from tears. For
although we were not forbidden to speak, yet anguish
and affliction suffered none of us to utter one word. For
the chords were so wonderfully made, yet none could
cut them, much less get them off his feet. Yet this comforted me: that still the future gain of many a one who
had now betaken himself to rest would prove very little
to his satisfaction. But we by one only night's penance
might expiate all our presumption: till at length in my
sorrowful thoughts I fell asleep.

As I slept, I had a dream, and though there be no
great matter in it, yet I esteem it not impertinent to
recount it. Methought I was upon an high mountain
and saw before me a great and large valley. In this valley

were gathered together an unspeakable multitude of people, each of which had at his head a thread by which he was hanged up towards heaven. Now one hung high, another low, some stood even quite upon the earth. But in the air there flew up and down an ancient man who had in his hand a pair of shears wherewith here he cut one or another's thread. He that was nigh the earth was so much the readier and would fall without noise; but when it happened to one of the high ones, he fell so that the earth quaked. To some it came to pass that their thread was so stretched that they came to the earth before the thread was cut. I took pleasure in this tumbling, and it joyed me at the heart when he who had over-exalted himself in the air, of his wedding, got so shameful a fall that it carried even some of his neighbours along with him. In like manner it also rejoiced me that he who had all this while kept himself near the earth could come down so fine and gently, that even his next men perceived it not. But, being now in my highest fit of jollity, I was unawares jogged by one of my fellow captives, upon which I was awaked and was very much discontented with him. Howbeit, I considered my dream, and recounted it to my brother who lay by me on the other side. He was not dissatisfied with it, but hoped some comfort might thereby be pretended. In such discourse we spent the remaining part of the night and, with longing, expected the day.

The Third Day

OW as soon as the lovely day was broken and the bright sun having raised himself above the hills had again betaken himself in the high heaven to his appointed office, my good champions began to rise out of their beds and leisurely to make themselves ready unto the inquisition. One after another they came again into the hall and, giving us a good morrow, demanded how we had slept. Having espied our bonds, there were some that reproved us for being so cowardly and that we had not, (much rather) as they, hazarded upon all adventures. Howbeit, some of them whose hearts still smote them made no loud cry of the business. We excused ourselves with our ignorance, hoping we should now soon be set at liberty and learn wit by this disgrace that they on the contrary had not yet altogether escaped and that perhaps their greatest danger was still to be expected.

At length, each one being again assembled, the trumpets began now again to sound and the kettle drums to beat as formerly, and we then imagined no other but that the Bridegroom was ready to present himself—which nevertheless was a huge mistake. For it was again the yesterday's Virgin who had arrayed herself all in red velvet and girded herself with a white scarf. Upon her head she had a green wreath of laurel, which hugely became her. Her train was now no more of small tapers, but consisted of two hundred men in harness, who were all (like her) clothed in red and white. As soon as they were alighted from the throne, she came straight to us prisoners and, after she had saluted us, said in few words:

"That some of you have been sensible of your wretched condition is hugely pleasing to my most mighty Lord, and he is also resolved you shall fare the better for it." And, having espied me in my habit, she laughed and spake:

"Good lack! Hast thou also submitted thyself to the yoke? I imagined thou wouldst have made thyself very smug."

With these words she caused my eyes to run over. Then she commanded we should be unbound and coupled together and placed in a station where we might well behold the scales. "For," said she, "it may yet fare better with them than with the presumptuous who yet stand here at liberty."

Meanwhile the scales (which were entirely of gold) were hung up in the midst of the hall. There was also a little table covered with red velvet and seven weights placed thereon. First of all stood a pretty great one, next four little ones, and lastly two great ones severally. These weights in proportion to their bulk were so heavy that no man can believe or comprehend it. Each of the harnessed men had a strong rope together with a naked sword. These she distributed according to the number of weights into seven bands. Out of every band, she chose one for their proper weight, and then again sprang up into her high throne. Then, as soon as she had made her reverence, with a very shrill tone she began thus to speak:

Who int'a painter's room does go
And nothing does of painting know,
Yet does in praying thereof pride it
Shall be of all the World derided.
Who into th' artists' order goes,
And thereunto was never chose,
Yet with pretense of skill does pride it,
Shall be of all the world derided.
Who at a wedding does appear,
And yet was ner'e intended there,
Yet does in coming highly pride it
Shall be of all the world derided.
Who now into this scale ascends,
The weights not proving his fast friends,
And that it bounces so does ride it
Shall be of all the world derided.

As soon as the Virgin had done speaking, one of the pages commanded each one to place himself according to his order and one after another to step in. One of the emperors made no scruple of this, but first of all bowed himself a little towards the Virgin, and afterwards in all his stately attire went up. Then each captain laid on his weight: to which (to the wonder of all) he stood unmoved. But the last was too heavy for him, so that forth he must go; and that with such anguish that (as it seemed to me) the Virgin herself had pity on him and beckoned to her people to hold their peace. Yet was the good emperor bound and delivered over to the sixth band.

Next came forth another emperor, who stepped haughtily into the scale and, having a great thick book under his gown, imagined not to fail. But being scarce able to abide the third weight, and being unmercifully slung down (his book in that affrightment slipping from him), all the soldiers began to laugh and he was delivered up bound to the third band. Thus it went also with some others of the emperors, who were all shamefully laughed at and captived.

After these came forth a little short man with a curled brown beard—an emperor, too—who after the usual reverence got up also. He held out so steadfastly that methought, had there been more weights ready, he would have outstood them. The Virgin immediately arose and bowed before him, causing him to put on a gown of red velvet, and at last reached him a branch of laurel, having good store of them upon her throne upon the steps whereof she willed him to sit down.

How after him it fared with the rest of the emperors, kings, and lords would be too long to recount, but I cannot leave unmentioned that few of those great personages held out. Howbeit, sundry eminent virtues (beyond my hopes) were found in many. One could stand out this, the second another, some two, some three, four or five, but few could attain to the just perfection—and everyone who failed was miserably laughed at by the bands.

After that the inquisition also passed over the gentry, the learned, the unlearned, and the rest. In each condition perhaps one, or it may be two, but for the most part none, was found perfect. It came at length to those honest gentlemen, the vagabond cheaters and rascally *Lapidem Spitalauficum*[1] makers, who were set upon the scale

---

1 Roughly, "false stone" (i.e., "snake oil"). Montgomery calls the term "a coined barbarism, in imitation of the professional jargon of the alchemical puffers and esoterists" (*Cross and Crucible*, 2:343).

with such scorn that I myself, for all my grief, was ready to burst my belly with laughing. Neither could the very prisoners themselves refrain: for the most part could not abide that severe trial but with whips and scourges were jerked out of the scale and led to the other prisoners, each to a suitable band. Thus of so great a throng so few remained that I am ashamed to discover their number. Howbeit, there were persons of quality also amongst them, who, notwithstanding, were (like the rest) honoured with velvet robes and wreaths of laurel.

The inquisition being completely finished, and none but we poor coupled hounds standing aside, at length one of the captains stepped forth and said, "Gracious madam, if it please your ladyship, let these poor men who acknowledged their misunderstanding be set upon the scale also—without their incurring any danger of penalty—and only for recreation's sake, if perchance anything that is right may be found amongst them."

In the first place, I was in great perplexity, for in my anguish this was my only comfort: that I was not to stand in such ignominy or be lashed out of the scale. For I nothing doubted but that many of the prisoners wished that they had stayed ten nights with us in the hall. Yet, since the Virgin consented, so it must be, and we being untied were one after another set up. Now, although the most part miscarried, yet they were neither laughed at nor scourged, but peaceably placed on one side. My companion was the fifth, and held out bravely, whereupon all—but especially the captain who made the request for us—applauded him and the Virgin shewed him the usual respect. After him again two more were dispatched in an instant.

I was the eighth. Now as soon as (with trembling) I stepped up, my companion who already sat by in his velvet looked friendly upon me and the Virgin herself smiled a little. But for as much as I outstayed all the weights, the Virgin commanded them to draw me up by force, wherefore three men moreover hung on the other side of the beam—and yet could nothing prevail. At once, one of the pages immediately stood up and cried out exceeding loud, "*THAT IS HE.*" Upon which the other replied, "Then let him gain his liberty," which the Virgin accorded.

Being received with due ceremonies, the choice was given me to release one of the captives, whosoever I pleased. I made no long deliberation, but elected the first emperor, whom I had long pitied: he was immediately set free and with all respect seated amongst us. Now the last being set up, the weights proved too heavy for him. In the meanwhile, the Virgin espied my roses, which I had taken out of my hat into my hands, and thereupon presently by her page graciously requested them of me, which I readily sent her. And so this first act was finished about ten in the forenoon. The trumpets began to sound again, which, nevertheless, we could not as yet see.

Meanwhile, the bands were to step aside with their prisoners and expect the judgment. A council of the seven captains and us was set, and the business was propounded by the Virgin as President, who desired each one to give his opinion concerning how the prisoners were to be dealt with. The first opinion was that they should all be put to death, some more severely than others (namely those who had presumptuously intruded themselves contrary to the express conditions). Others would have them kept close prisoners. Both options pleased neither the President nor me. At length by one of the emperors (the same whom I had freed), my companion, and myself the affair was brought to this point: that first of the principal lords should with a befitting respect be led out of the castle. Others might be carried out, somewhat more scornfully. These should be stripped and caused to run out naked. The fourth with rods, whips, or dogs should be hunted out. Those who the day before willingly surrendered themselves might be suffered to depart without any blame. Last of all, those presumptuous ones and they who behaved themselves so unseemly at dinner the day before should be punished in body and life according to each man's demerle.[2]

This opinion pleased the Virgin well and obtained the upper hand. There was, moreover, another dinner vouchsafed them, which they were soon acquainted with. But the execution was deferred till twelve at noon. Herewith the senate arose and the Virgin together with them. Attendants returned to her usual quarter. But the uppermost table in the room was allotted to us, they requesting us to take it in good part till the business were fully dispatched. And then we should he conducted to the Lord Bridegroom and the Bride, with which we were at present well content.

In the meantime, the prisoners were again brought into the hall, each man seated according to his quality. They were likewise enjoined to behave themselves somewhat more civilly than they had done the day

---

2 "Misdeeds."

before—which admonishment they needed not, for they had already put up their pipes. And this I can boldly say, not with flattery, but in the love of truth, that commonly those persons who were of the highest rank best understood how to behave themselves in so unexpected a misfortune. Their treatment was but indifferent, yet with respect; neither could they yet see their attendants, who were now to us visible, whereat I was exceeding joyful.

Now, although Fortune had exalted us, we took not upon us more than the rest, advising them to be of good cheer that the event would not be so ill. Although they would gladly have understood the sentence of us, yet we were so deeply obliged that none durst open his mouth about it. Nevertheless, we comforted them as well as we could, drinking with them to try if the wine might make them anything cheerfuller.

Our table was covered with red velvet beset with drinking-cups of pure silver and gold, which the rest could not behold without amazement and very great anguish. But, e're we had seated ourselves, in came the two pages presenting everyone in the Bridegroom's behalf the Golden Fleece with a Flying Lion, requesting us to wear them at the table, and as became us, to observe the reputation and dignity of the Order which His Majesty had now vouchsafed us, and should suddenly be ratified with suitable ceremonies.[3] This we

---

3 Yates makes quite a case for the influence of England's Royal Order of the Garter on the similar order in the *CW*. It is a case, however, that seems a bit tenuous. See Frances A. Yates, *The Rosicrucian Enlightenment*, 68–69.

received with profoundest submission, promising obediently to perform whatsoever His Majesty should please. Besides these, the noble page had a schedule wherein we were set down in order. For my part, I should not otherwise be desirous to conceal my place, if perchance it might not be interpreted to pride, which yet is expressly against the fourth weight.[4]

Now because our entertainment was exceeding stately, we demanded one of the pages whether we might not have leave to send some choice bit to our friends and acquaintances. Making no difficulty of it, everyone sent plentifully to his acquaintances by the waiters, howbeit they saw none of them. And, forasmuch as they knew not whence it came, I was myself desirous to carry somewhat to one of them; but as soon as I was risen, one of the waiters was presently at my elbow, saying he desired me to take friendly warning: for in case one of the pages had seen it, it would have come to the King's ear—and he would certainly have taken it amiss of me. But since none had observed it but himself, he purposed not to betray me, save that I ought for the time to come to have better regard to the dignity of the order. With these words the servant did really so astonish me that for a long time after I scarce moved upon my seat, yet I returned him thanks for his faithful warning as well as in haste and affrightment I was able.

Soon after the drums began to beat again—to which

4 Since pride is the sin committed here, the weights would then represent the Seven Virtues (humility, kindness, abstinence, chastity, patience, liberality, and diligence) which oppose the Seven Deadly Sins (pride, envy, gluttony, lust, anger, greed, sloth). The fourth weight, then, represents humility—which many of the artists in the contest certainly lack!

we were already accustomed. We well knew they announced the Virgin, wherefore we prepared ourselves to receive her who was now coming in with her usual train in her high seat, one of the pages bearing before her a very tall goblet of gold and the other a patent in parchment. Being now after a marvelous artificial manner alighted from the seat, she took the goblet from the page and presented the same in the King's behalf, saying that it was brought us from His Majesty and that in honour of him we should cause it to go round. Upon the cover of this goblet stood Fortune curiously cast in gold, who had in her hand a red flying ensign. For this reason, I drunk somewhat the more sadly, as having been but too well acquainted with Fortune's waywardness.

But the Virgin, as well as we, was adorned with the Golden Fleece and Lion, whence I observed that perhaps she was the President of the Order. At this, we demanded of her how the Order might be named. She answered that it was not yet seasonable to discover it, till the affair with the prisoners were dispatched. Therefore, their eyes were still held; and what had hitherto happened to us was to them only for an offence and scandal, although it were to be accounted as nothing in regard of the honour that attended us. Hereupon she began to distinguish the patent which the other page held into two different parts, out of which about thus much was read before the first company: that they should confess that they had too lightly given credit to false fictitious books, had assumed too much to themselves, and so came into this castle, albeit they were never invited into it, and perhaps the most part had presented themselves with design to make their markets here and afterwards to live in the greater pride and lordliness. Thus one had seduced another and plunged him into this disgrace and ignominy, wherefore they were deservedly to be soundly punished.

This they with great humility readily acknowledged, and gave their hands upon it. After this a severe check was given to the rest, much to this purpose: that they very well knew (and were in their consciences convinced) that they had forged false fictitious books, had befooled others and cheated them, and thereby had diminished regal dignity amongst all. They knew in like manner what ungodly deceitful figures they had made use of, insomuch as they spared not even the Divine Trinity, but accustomed themselves to cheat people all the country over. It was also now as clear as day with what practices they had endeavoured to ensnare the true guests and introduce the ignorant. In like manner, it was manifest to all the world that they wallowed in open whoredom, adultery, gluttony, and other uncleannesses—all which was against the express orders of our kingdom. In brief, they knew they had disparaged Kingly Majesty, even amongst the common sort, and therefore they should confess themselves to be manifest convicted vagabond-cheaters, knaves, and rascals, whereby they deserved to be cashiered from the company of civil people and severely to be punished.

The good artists were loath to come to this confession. Not only did the Virgin herself threaten and swear their death but the other party also vehemently raged at them and unanimously cried out that they had most wickedly seduced them out of the light. They, at length, to prevent a huge misfortune confessed the same with

dolour, and yet withal alleged that what had herein happened was not to be animadverted upon them in the
worst sense. For inasmuch as the lords were absolutely
resolved to get into the castle and had promised great
sums of money to that effect, each one had used all craft
to seize upon something, and so things were brought to
that pass—as was now manifest before their eyes. But
that it succeeded not, they in their opinion had dis-
deserved no more than the lords themselves. As who
should have had so much understanding as to consider
that in case anyone had been sure of getting in, he
would not, in so great peril, for the sake of a slight gain
have clambered over the wall with them. Their books
also sold so mightily that whoever had no other means
to maintain himself was fain to engage in such a
cosenage. They hoped, moreover, that if a right judgement were made they should be found no way to have
miscarried, as having behaved themselves towards the
lords as became servants upon their earnest entreaty.

Answer was made them that his Royal Majesty had
determined to punish all and every man, albeit one
more severely than another. For although what had
been alleged by them was partly true, and therefore the
lords should not wholly be indulged, yet they had good
reason to prepare themselves for death who had so presumptuously obtruded themselves and perhaps seduced
the more ignorant against their will. Likewise, they who
with false books had violated Royal Majesty as the others might be evinced out of their very writings and
books.

Hereupon many began most piteously to lament, cry,
weep, entreat, and prostrate themselves: all which, not-

withstanding, could avail them nothing. I much marveled how the Virgin could be so resolute, when yet their misery caused our eyes to run over and moved our compassion (although the most part of them had procured us much trouble and vexation). She presently dispatched her page, who brought with him all the cuirassiers which had this day been appointed at the scales. They were commanded each of them to take his own to him, and in an orderly procession, so as still each cuirassiers should go with one of the prisoners to conduct them into her great garden. At which time each one so exactly recognised his own man that I marveled at it. Leave also was likewise given to my yesterday companions to go out into the garden unbound and to be present at the execution of the sentence.

As soon as every man was come forth, the Virgin mounted up into her high throne, requesting us to sit down upon the steps and to appear at the judgment. This we refused not, but left all standing upon the table (except the goblet, which the Virgin committed to the page's keeping) and went forth in our robes upon the throne, which of itself moved so gently as if we had passed in the air till in this manner we came into the garden, where we arose altogether.

This garden[5] was not extraordinary curious, though it

---

5 In alchemy, the Garden of the Philosophers is the secret vessel in which the alchemical work is accomplished. Arnoldus Villanova's *Rosarium philosophorum* (1550) utilizes this imagery to a significant degree. See Abraham, *Dictionary of Alchemical Imagery*, 84. In scripture, the Song of Songs describes the bride in similar terms: "You are an enclosed garden, my sister, my bride, an enclosed garden, a fountain sealed" (4:12).

THE CHYMICAL WEDDING

pleased me that the trees were planted in so good order. In addition, there ran in it a most costly fountain adorned with wonderful figures and inscriptions, and strange characters, (which, God willing, I shall mention in a future book). In this garden was raised a wooden scaffold hung about with curiously painted figured coverlets. Now there were four galleries made one over another. The first was more glorious than any of the rest, and therefore covered with a white taffeta curtain so that at that time we could not perceive who was behind it. The second was empty and uncovered. The two last were covered with red and blue taffeta.

Now as soon as we were come to the scaffold, the Virgin bowed herself down to the ground, at which we were mightily terrified: for we might easily guess that the King and Queen must not be far off. We having duly performed our reverence, the Virgin led us up by the winding-stairs into the second gallery where she placed herself uppermost and us in our former order. But how the emperor whom I had released behaved himself towards me, both at this time as also before at the table, I cannot, without slander of wicked tongues, well relate. For he might well imagine in what anguish and solicitude he now should have been, in case he were at present to attend the judgment with such ignominy, and that only through me had he now attained such dignity and worthiness.

Meanwhile, the Virgin who first of all brought me the invitation and whom hitherto I had never since seen stepped in. First she gave one blast upon her trumpet, and then with a very loud voice declared the sentence in this manner:

"The King's Majesty, my Most Gracious Lord, could from his heart wish that all and everyone here assembled had upon His Majesty's invitation presented themselves so qualified as that they might (to his honour) with greatest frequency have adorned this his appointed nuptial and joyful feast. But since it hath otherwise pleased Almighty God, His Majesty hath not whereat to murmur, but must be forced, contrary to his own inclination, to abide by the ancient and laudable constitutions of this kingdom. But now, that His Majesty's innate clemency may be celebrated over all the world, he hath thus far absolutely dealt with his council and estates that the usual sentence shall be considerably lenified.

"Therefore, in the first place he is willing to vouchsafe to the lords and potentates not only their lives entirely, but also freely and frankly to dismiss them, friendly and courteously entreating your lordships not at all to take it in evil part that you cannot be present at His Majesty's feast of honour, but to remember that there is notwithstanding more imposed upon your lordships by God Almighty (who in the distribution of his gifts hath an incomprehensible consideration) than you can duly and easily sustain.[6] Neither is your reputation hereby prejudiced, although you be rejected by this our Order, since we cannot at once all of us do all things. But for as much as your lordships have been seduced by base rascals, it shall not on their part pass unrevenged.

6 "And unto whomsoever much is given, of him much shall be required: and to whom they have committed much, of him they will demand the more" (Luke 12:48).

Furthermore, His Majesty resolveth shortly to communicate with your lordships a *Catalogue of Hereticks* or *Index Expurgatorius* that you may henceforward be able with better judgment to discern between the Good and the Evil. And because His Majesty e're long also purposeth to rummage his library and offer up the seductive writings to Vulcan, he friendly, humbly, and courteously entreats every one of your lordships to put the same in execution with your own, whereby it is to be hoped that all evil and mischief may for the time to come be remedied. And you are withal to be admonished never henceforth so inconsiderately to covet an entrance hither, lest the former excuse of seducers be taken from you, and you fall into disgrace and contempt with all men. In fine, for as much as the estates of the land have still somewhat to demand of your lordships, His Majesty hopes that no man will think much to redeem himself with a chain or what else he hath about him, and so in friendly manner to depart from us, and through our safe conduct to betake himself home again.

"The others who stood not at the first, third, and fourth weights, His Majesty will not so lightly dismiss. But that they also may now experience His Majesty's gentleness, it is his command to strip them stark naked and so send them forth.

"Those who in the second and fifth weight were found too light shall besides stripping be noted with one, two, or more brand-marks, according as each one was lighter, or heavier.

"They who were drawn up by the, sixth or seventh, and not by the rest, shall be somewhat more graciously dealt withal, and so forward." (For up to every combination there was a certain punishment ordained which were here too long to recount.)

"They who yesterday separated themselves freely of their own record, shall go out at liberty without any blame.

"Finally, the convicted vagabond-cheaters who could move up none of the weights shall, as occasion serves, be punished in body and life with the sword, halter, water, and rods. And such execution of judgement shall be inviolably observed as an example unto others."

Herewith our Virgin broke her wand (while the other who read the sentence blew her trumpet) and stepped with most profound reverence towards those who stood behind the curtain.

But here I cannot omit to discover somewhat to the reader concerning the number of our prisoners: of whom those who weighed one, were seven; those who weighted two, were twenty one; they who three, thirty five; they who four, thirty five; those who five, twenty one; those who six, seven; but he that came to the seventh, and yet could not well raise it, he was only one, and, indeed, the same whom I released. Of them who wholly failed there were many, but of those who drew all the weights from the ground but few. And these, as they stood severally before us, so I diligently numbered and noted them down in my table-book. And it is very admirable that amongst all those who weighed anything, none was equal to another. For although amongst those who weighed three, there were thirty five, yet one of them weighed the first, second, and third, another the third, fourth, and fifth, a third, the fifth, sixth, and seventh and so on. It is likewise very wonderful that

amongst one hundred twenty six who weighed anything, none was equal to another. I would very willingly
name them all, with each man's weight, were it not as
yet forbidden me. But I hope it may hereafter be published with the interpretation.

Now this Judgment being read over, the lords in the
first place were well satisfied, because in such severity
they durst not look for a mild sentence. For which cause
they gave more than they were desired, and each one
redeemed himself with chains, jewels, gold, monies and
other things—as much as they had about them—and
with reverence took leave. Now, although the King's
servants were forbidden to jeer any at his going away,
yet some unlucky birds could not hold laughing, and
certainly it was sufficiently ridiculous to see them pack
away with such speed without once looking behind
them. Some desired that the promised catalogue might
with the first be dispatched after them, and then they
would take such order with their books as should be
pleasing to His Majesty, and this was again assured. At
the door was given to each of them out of a cup *Oblivio-
nis Haustus*,[7] that so he might have no further memory
of misfortune.

After these the volunteers departed, who because of
their ingenuity were suffered to pass but yet so as never
to return again in the same fashion. But if to them (as
likewise to the others) anything further were revealed,
then they should be welcome guests.

Meanwhile, the others were being stripped, in which
also an inequality (according to each man's demerit) was

7 "Draft of Forgetfulness" or "Draught of Oblivion."

observed. Some were sent away naked, without other hurt. Others were driven out with small bells. Some were scourged forth. In brief, the punishments were so various that I am not able to recount them all. In the end it came to the last, with whom somewhat a longer time was spent, for whilst some were hanging, some beheading, some forced to leap into the water, and the rest otherwise dispatching, much time was consumed. Verily, at this execution my eyes ran over, not indeed in regard of the punishment, which they otherwise for their impudence well deserved, but in contemplation of humane blindness, in that we are continually busying ourselves in that which ever since the first Fall hath been hitherto sealed upon us.

Thus the garden, which so lately was quite full, was soon emptied so that besides the soldiers there was not a man left. As soon as this was done, and silence had been kept for the space of five minutes, there came forward a beautiful snow-white unicorn with a golden collar (having in it certain letters) about his neck. In the same place he bowed himself down upon both his forefeet, as if hereby he had shown honour to the lion who stood so immovably upon the fountain, that I took him to be of stone or brass. Immediately the lion took the naked sword which he bare in his paw and brake it in the middle in two, the pieces whereof to my thinking sunk into the fountain. After this he so long roared until a white dove brought a branch of olive in her bill, which the lion devoured in an instant, and so was quieted. And so the unicorn returned to his place with joy.

Hereupon our Virgin led us down again by the winding-stairs from the scaffold, and so we again made our reverence towards the curtain. We were to wash our hands and heads in the fountain, and there a little while to wait in our order till the King, through a certain secret gallery, were again returned into his hall. And then we also with choice music, pomp, state, and pleasant discourse were conducted into our former lodging. This was done about four in the afternoon.

But that in the meanwhile the time might not seem too long to us, the Virgin bestowed on each of us a noble page, not only richly habited, but also exceeding learned. They could so aptly discourse upon all subjects that we had good reason to be ashamed of ourselves. These were commanded to lead us up and down the castle (yet not into certain places) and, if possible, to shorten the time according to our desire. Meanwhile, the Virgin took leave with this consolation: that at supper she would be with us again, and after that celebrate the ceremonies of the hanging up of the weights, requesting that we would in patience wait till the next day, for on the morrow we must be presented to the King.

She being thus departed from us, each of us did what best pleased him. One part viewed the excellent paintings, which they copied out for themselves, and considered also what the wonderful characters might signify. Others were fain to recruit themselves again with meat and drink. I, indeed, caused my page to conduct me (together with my companion) up and down the castle, of which walk it will never repent me as long as I have a day to live. For, besides many other glorious antiquities, the Royal Sepulcher was also shewed me, by which I learned more than is extant in all books. There in the same place stands also the glorious phoenix (of which

two years since I published a particular small discourse)
and am resolved (in case this my narration shall prove
useful) to set forth several and peculiar treatises concerning the lion, eagle, griffin, falcon, and other like,
together with their draughts and inscriptions. It grieves
me also for my other consorts that they neglected such
precious treasures. And yet I cannot but think it was the
special will of God it should be so. I, indeed, reaped the
most benefit by my page, for according as each one's
genius lay, so he led his entrusted into the quarters and
places which were pleasing to him. Now the keys here-
unto belonging were committed to my page, and therefore this good fortune happened to me before the rest:
for although he invited others to come in, yet they,
imagining such tombs to be only in the churchyard,
thought they should well enough get thither whenever
anything was to be seen there. Neither shall these monuments (as both of us copied and transcribed them) be
withheld from my thankful scholars.

The other thing that was shewed us two was the noble
library as it was altogether before the Reformation.[8] Of
the library (albeit it rejoices my heart as often as I call it
to mind) I have so much the less to say because the catalogue thereof is very shortly to be published. At the

---

8 In this allegedly Protestant text the library condition *intacta* is celebrated as a wonder and its loss lamented—and followed with sarcasm:
"many of these were to be burnt, that so even their memory may be blotted out from amongst the righteous." Much as Ben Jonson does in a number of his plays, Andreae here rips on shows of piety among the
"righteous" Reformers, echoing the manner in which he also lambastes
the pride of scholars and alchemists earlier. He was nothing if not hyper-
aware of pretense.

entry of this room stands a great book, the like whereof I never saw, in which all the figures, rooms, portals, also all the writings, riddles, and the like to be seen in the whole castle are delineated. Although we have made some promise concerning this also, yet at present I must contain myself and first learn to know the world better. In every book stands its author painted. As I understood, many of these were to be burnt, that so even their memory may be blotted out from amongst the righteous.

Now, having taken a full view hereof and being scarce gotten forth, another page came running to us, and, having whispered somewhat in our page's ear, he delivered up the keys to him who immediately carried them up the winding-stairs. Our page was very much out of countenance at this, and, we setting hard upon him with entreaties, he declared to us that the King's Majesty would by no means permit that either of the two, namely the library and sepulchers, should be seen by any man. Therefore he besought us, as we tendered his life, to discover it to no man, he having already utterly denied it. At this, both of us stood hovering between joy and fear. Nevertheless, it continued in silence, and no man made further inquiry about it. Thus in both places we consumed three hours, which does not at all repent me.

Now, although it had already struck seven, yet nothing was hitherto given us to eat, howbeit our hunger was easily to be abated by constant revivings and I could be well content to fast all my life long with such entertainment. About this time the curious fountains, mines, and all kind of art-shops[9] were also shown us, of which

9 That is, workshops, studios.

there was none but surpassed all our arts, though they should all be melted into one mass. All their chambers were built in a semicircle, that so they might have before their eyes the costly clockwork which was erected upon a fair turret in the center and regulate themselves according to the course of the planets, which were to be seen on it in a glorious manner. And hence I could easily conjecture wherein our artists failed, howbeit it's none of my duty to inform them.

At length I came into a spacious room (shown indeed to the rest a great while before) in the middle whereof stood a terrestrial globe whose diameter contained thirty feet, near half of it, except a little which was covered with the steps, that was let into the earth. Two men might readily turn this globe about with all its furniture so that no more of it was to be seen but was above the horizon. Now, although I could easily conceive that this was of some special use, yet could I not understand whereto those ringlets of gold (which were upon it in several places) served. At this my page laughed and advised me to view them more closely. In brief, I found there my native country noted with gold also; whereupon my companion sought his and found that so, too. Now, for as much as the same happened in like manner to the rest who stood by, the page told us of a certain that it was yesterday declared to the King's Majesty by their old Atlas (so is the astronomer named)[10] that all the gilded points did exactly answer to their native countries, according as had been shown of each of them.

10 Note the joke: Atlas in Classical mythology is the titan who holds up the sky. The astrologer, likewise, "holds up the sky" in his way.

Thereupon, as soon as he perceived that I undervalued myself (even though there stood a point upon my native country), he also moved one of the captains to entreat for us that we should be set upon the scale (without our peril) at all adventures, especially seeing one of our native countries had a notable good mark. And truly it was not without cause that he, the page who had the greatest power of all the rest, was bestowed on me. For this I then returned him thanks and immediately looked more diligently upon my native country and found, moreover, that besides the ringlet there were also certain delicate streaks upon it, which nevertheless I would not be thought to speak to my own praise or glory. I saw much more too upon this globe than I am willing to discover. Let each man take into consideration why every city produceth not a philosopher.

After this he led us quite into the globe, which was thus made: on the sea (there being a large square besides it) was a tablet whereon stood three dedications and the author's name. This a man might gently lift up and by a little joined board go into the center, which was capable of four persons, being nothing but a round board whereon we could sit and at ease by broad daylight (it was now already dark) contemplate the stars. To my thinking, they were pure carbuncles which glittered in such an agreeable order and moved so gallantly that I had scarce any mind ever to go out again, as the page afterwards told the Virgin, and with which she often twitted me. Indeed, it was already supper time, and I had so much amused myself in the globe that I was almost the last at table.

I made no longer delay, but having again put on my

gown (which I had before laid aside) and stepping to the table, the waiters treated me with so much reverence and honour that for shame I durst not look up. And so unawares, I permitted the Virgin, who attended me on one side, to stand, which she soon perceiving twitched me by the gown and so led me to the table. To speak any further concerning the music or the rest of that magnificent entertainment, I hold it needless, both because it is not possible sufficiently to express it and I have already reported it according to my power. In brief, there was nothing there but art and amenity. After we had each to other related our employment since noon (howbeit, not a word was spoken of the library and monuments) being already merry with the wine, the Virgin began thus:

"My lords, I have a great contention with one of my sisters. In our chamber we have an eagle and we cherish him with such diligence that each of us is desirous to be his best beloved, and upon that score have many a squabble. On a day we concluded to go both together to him, and toward whom he should shew himself most friendly, hers should he properly be. This we did, and I (as commonly) bare in my hand a branch of laurel, but my sister had none. Now as soon as he espied us both, he immediately gave my sister another branch which he had in his beak, and offered at mine, which I gave him. Now each of us hereupon imagined herself to be best beloved of him. Which way am I to resolve myself?"

This modest proposal of the Virgin pleased us all mighty well, and each one would gladly have heard the solution; but, inasmuch as they all looked upon me and desired to have the beginning from me, my mind was so extremely confounded that I knew not what else to do with it but propound another in its stead. Therefore, I said, "Gracious Lady, your Ladyship's question were easily to be resolved if one thing did not perplex me. I had two companions, both which loved me exceedingly. Now they, being doubtful which of them was most dear to me, concluded to run to me unawares, and that he whom I should then embrace should be the right. This they did, yet one of them could not keep pace with the other, so he stayed behind and wept. The other I embraced with amazement. When they had afterwards discovered the business to me, I knew not how to resolve myself and have hitherto let it rest in this manner until I may find some good advice herein."

The Virgin wondered at it, and well observed whereabout I was, whereupon she replied, "Well, then, let us both be quit" and then desired the solution from the rest. But I had already made them wise. Wherefore the next began thus:

"In the city where I live, a virgin was lately condemned to death. But the judge, being something pitiful towards her, caused it to be proclaimed that if any man desired to become the virgin's champion he should have free leave to do it. Now she had two lovers. The one presently made himself ready and came into the lists to expect his adversary. Afterwards the other also presented himself, but coming somewhat too late he resolved nevertheless to fight and willingly suffer himself to be vanquished, that so the virgin's life might be preserved, which also succeeded according. Whereupon each challenged her. Now, my lords, instruct me: to which of them of right belongeth she?"

The Virgin could hold no longer, but said, "I thought

to have gained much information—and am myself gotten into the net!—but yet would gladly hear whether there be any more behind."

"Yes, that there is," answered the third. "A stranger adventure hath not been yet recounted then that which happened to myself. In my youth I loved a worthy maid. Now that this my love might attain its wished end, I was fain to make use of an ancient matron, who easily brought me to her. Now it happened that the maid's brethren came in upon us just as we three were together, and they were in such a rage that they would have taken my life. But upon my vehement supplication they at length forced me to swear to take each of them for a year as my wedded wife. Now tell me, my lords, should I take the old or the young one first?"

We all laughed sufficiently at this riddle, and though some of them muttered one to another thereupon, yet none would undertake to unfold it. Hereupon the fourth began:

"In a certain city there dwelt an honourable lady who was beloved of all, but especially by a young nobleman, who would needs be too importunate with her. At length she gave him this determination: that in case he would, in a cold winter, lead her into a fair green garden of roses, then he should obtain; but, if not, he must resolve never to see her more. The nobleman travelled into all countries to find such a man as might perform this, till at length he lit upon a little old man that promised to do it for him if he would assure him of half his estate. He, having consented to the other, was as good as his word. At this he invited the foresaid lady home to his garden, where, contrary to her expectation, she found all things green, pleasant, and warm. Remembering her promise, she only requested that she might once more return to her lord, to whom with sighs and tears she bewailed her lamentable condition. But for as much as he sufficiently perceived her faithfulness, he dispatched her back to her lover, who had so dearly purchased her, that she might give him satisfaction. This husband's integrity did so mightily affect the nobleman that he thought it a sin to touch so honest a wife, so he sent her home again with honour to her lord. Now the little man, perceiving such faith in both these, would not, how poor soever he were, be the least, but restored the nobleman all his goods again and went his way. Now, my lords, I know not which of these persons may have shown the greatest ingenuity."[11]

Here our tongues were quite cut off. Neither would the Virgin make any other reply, but only that another should go on. Wherefore the fifth without delay began:

"My lords, I desire not to make long work. Who hath the greater joy? He that beholdeth what he loveth, or he that only thinketh on it?"

"He that beholdeth it," said the Virgin.

"Nay," answered I.

Hereupon arose a contest, wherefore the sixth called out:

"My lords, I am to take a wife. Now I have before me a maid, a married wife, and a widow. Ease me of this doubt, and I will afterwards help to order the rest."[12]

"It goes well there," replied the seventh, "where a

---

11 The tale derives from Boccaccio's *Decameron*, 10.5.

12 Likewise from Boccaccio's *Decameron*, 10.4.

man hath his choice, but with me the case is otherwise.[13] In my youth I loved a fair and virtuous virgin
from the bottom of my heart, and she me in like manner. Howbeit, because of her friend's denial, we could
not come together in wedlock. Whereupon she was
married to another, yet an honest and discreet person,
who maintained her honourably and with affection until
she came into the pains of childbirth. This went so hard
with her that all thought she had been dead, so with
much state and great mourning she was interred. Now,
I thought with myself: 'During her life thou couldst
have no part in this woman, but yet now dead as she is
thou mayst embrace and kiss her sufficiently.' Whereupon I took my servant with me, who dug her up by
night. Now, having opened the coffin and locked her in
my arms and feeling about her heart, I found still some
little motion in it, which increased more and more from
my warmth, till at last I perceived that she was indeed
still alive. Wherefore I quietly bare her home, and after
I had warmed her chilled body with a costly bath of
herbs, I committed her to my mother until she brought

13 The following story has much in common with William Shakespeare's telling of *Romeo and Juliet*, a decidedly alchemical play. In alchemy, the chymical king and queen are often depicted as entombed/bedded
together as a stage in accomplishing the Alchemical Work (the *coninunc-
tio*). This, of course, transpires in *Romeo and Juliet*. It is also important to
note that Shakespeare's play ends with the fathers of Romeo and Juliet
promising to erect statues of each other's child, transforming the star-
crossed lovers into *pure gold*, a chiastic figure that would have made any
late-16th century alchemist smile. As Abraham points out, the chamber
that serves as both tomb and bridal bed is the site of the chemical wedding
itself. See *Dictionary of Alchemical Imagery*, 36–38.

forth a fair son, whom (as the mother) I caused faithfully to be nursed. After two days (she being then in a
mighty amazement), I discovered to her all the fore-
passed affair, requesting her that for the time to come
she would live with me as a wife, against which she thus
excepted, in case it should be grievous to her husband
who had well and honourably maintained her. But, if it
could otherwise be, she was the present obliged in love
to one as well as the other. Now, after two months
(being then to make a journey elsewhere) I invited her
husband as a guest, and, amongst other things,
demanded of him whether if his deceased wife should
come home again he could be content to receive her. He
affirming it with tears and lamentations, at length I
brought him his wife together with his son, and an
account of all the fore-passed business, entreating him
to ratify with his consent my fore-purposed espousals.
After a long dispute he could not beat me from my
right, but was fain to leave me the wife. But still the
contest was about the son."

Here the Virgin interrupted him and said, "It makes
me wonder how you could double the afflicted man's
grief."

"How," answered he, "was I not then concerned?"

Upon this there arose a dispute amongst us, yet the
most part affirmed that he had done but right.

"Nay," said he, "I freely returned him both his wife
and son. Now tell me, my lords, was my honesty or this
man's joy the greater?"

These words had so mightily cheered the Virgin that
(as if it had been for the sake of these two) she caused a
health to go round. After this the rest of the proposals

went on somewhat perplexedly, so that I could not retain them all. Yet this comes to my mind: that one said that a few years before he had seen a physician who bought a parcel of wood against winter, with which he warmed himself all winter long. As soon as the spring returned, he sold the very same wood again, and so had the use of it for nothing.

"Here must needs be skill," said the Virgin, "but the time is now past."

"Yea," replied my companion, "whoever understands not how to resolve all the riddles may give each man notice of it by a proper messenger. I conceive he will not be denied."

At this time they began to say grace, and we arose altogether from the table, rather satisfied and merry than glutted. It were to be wished that all invitations and feastings were thus to be kept.

Having now taken some few turns up and down the hall again, the Virgin asked us whether we desired to begin the wedding.

"Yes," said one noble and virtuous lady; whereupon she privately dispatched a page, and yet in the meantime proceeded in discourse with us.

In brief, she was already become so familiar with us that I adventured and requested her name. The Virgin smiled at my curiosity, but yet was not moved, but replied, "My name contains five and fifty, and yet hath only eight letters. The third is the third part of the fifth which added to the sixth will produce a number whose root shall exceed the third itself by just the first: and it is the half of the fourth. Now the fifth and the seventh are equal. The last and the first are also equal, and make with the second as much as the sixth hath, which contains just four more than the third tripled. Now tell me, my lord, how am I called?"

The answer was intricate enough to me, yet I left not off so, but said, "Noble and virtuous Lady, may I not obtain one only letter?"

"Yea," said she, "that may well be done."

"What then," replied I again, "may the seventh contain?"

"It contains," said she, "as many as there are lords here."

With this I was content and easily found her name. She was well pleased, with assurance that much more should yet be revealed to us.[14]

In the meantime, certain virgins had made themselves ready and came in with great ceremony. First of all, two youths carried lights before them. One of them was of a jocund countenance, sprightly eyes and gentle propor-

---

14 Andreae was fond of tricks and red herrings and this puzzle is no exception. The Virgin's clue suggests that the seventh letter (which is the same as the fifth) is 9, which would make the letter I (the ninth letter in the alphabet). Knowing this, the rest is easily solved. Since the third letter is a third of the fifth, 3 is C. The sixth letter, being four more than the third tripled ($4 + 3 \times 3 = 13$), the letter is M. The third is a third of the fifth, which added to the sixth will produce a number the root of which exceeds the third by the first and is half of the fourth, which makes for 8. The second letter, finally, is equal to the sixth (M or 13) minus the first or last ($13 - 1$), which makes L. Thus the Virgin's name is ALCHIMIA. The alert reader will notice that the sum of the numbers of ALCHIMIA ($1 + 12 + 3 + 8 + 9 + 13 + 9 + 1$) equals 56, and not 55 as the Virgin says. This is authorial sleight of hand at its best (just as the Virgin tricks most of the alchemists throughout the tale), for, as Bleiler points out, "the numerical total of the letters in her name is completely irrelevant to solving the puzzle" (Bleiler, "Johann Valentine Andreae, Fantasist and Utopist," 25).

tion. The other looked something angrily; whatever he would have must be, as I afterwards perceived.

After them first followed four virgins. One looked shame-facedly towards the earth, very humble in behavior. The second also was a modest, bashful virgin. The third as she entered the room seemed amazed at something; and as I understood she cannot well abide where there is too much mirth. The fourth brought with her certain small wreaths, thereby to manifest her kindness and liberality.[15] After these four came two which were somewhat more gloriously appareled; they saluted us courteously. One of them had a gown of sky colour spangled with golden stars. The other's was green, beautified with red and white stripes. On their heads they had thin flying tiffaties,[16] which did most becomingly adorn them. At last came one alone, who had on her head a coronet, but rather looked up towards heaven than towards earth.[17] We all thought it had been the Bride, but were much mistaken (although otherwise in honour, riches, and state she much surpassed the Bride—and she afterwards ruled the whole wedding).[18]

15 The first four virgins suggest the Four Cardinal Virtues: Prudence, Temperance, Fortitude, and Justice.

16 Kerchiefs.

17 The noble lady, according to both Montgomery and Rudolf Steiner, is THEOLOGIA. See *Cross and Crucible*, 2:383 and Rudolf Steiner, "*The Chymical Wedding of Christian Rosenkreutz*," trans. Carlo Pietzner, in *A Christian Rosenkreutz Anthology*, ed. Paul M. Allen in collaboration with Carlo Pietzner (Blauvelt, NY: Rudolf Steiner Publications, 1968), 19–59, at 44.

18 The last three virgins represent Astronomy, Natural Philosophy, and Theology, the mastery of which needs to be accompanied by the Four Cardinal Virtues.

Now on this occasion we all followed our Virgin and fell down on our knees, howbeit the Bride shewed herself extreme humble, offering everyone her hand and admonishing us not to be too much surprised at this (for this was one of her smallest bounties) but to lift up our eyes to our Creator and learn hereby to acknowledge His Omnipotency and so proceed in our enterprised course, employing this grace to the praise of God and the good of man. In sum, her words were quite different from those of our Virgin, who was somewhat more worldly. They pierced even through my bones and marrow. "And thou," said she further to me, "hast received more than others, that thou also make a larger return." This to me was a very strange sermon.

As soon as we saw the virgins with the music, we imagined we must presently fall to dancing, but that time was not as yet come. Now the weights, whereof mention hath been before made, stood still in the same place. Then the Queen (I yet knew not who she was) commanded each virgin to take up one, but to our Virgin she gave her own, which was the last and greatest, and commanded us to follow behind. Our majesty was then somewhat abated, for I well observed that our Virgin was but too good for us and that we were not so highly reputed as we ourselves were almost in part willing to phantasy. So we went behind in our order and were brought into the first chamber where our Virgin in the first place hung up the Queen's weight, during which an excellent spiritual hymn was sung.

There was nothing costly in this room, save only certain curious little prayer books which should never be missing. In the midst was erected a pulpit, very convenient for prayer, wherein the Queen kneeled down. About her we were all fain to kneel and pray after the Virgin, who read out of a book that this wedding might tend to the honour of God and our own benefit. Afterwards we came into the second chamber, where the first virgin hung up her weight also, and so forward till all the ceremonies were finished. Hereupon the Queen again presented her hand to everyone and departed thence with her virgin.

Our President stayed yet a while with us. But because it had been already two hours night, she would no longer detain us. Methought she was glad of our company, yet she bid us good night and wished us quiet rest, and so departed friendly from us, although unwillingly. Our pages were well instructed in their business and therefore shewed every man his chamber and stayed also with us upon another pallet, that in case we wanted anything we might make use of them. My chamber (of the rest I am not able to speak) was royally furnished with rare tapestries and hung about with paintings. But above all things I delighted in my page, who was so excellently spoken and experienced in the arts that he yet spent me another hour, and it was half an hour after three when first I fell asleep.

And this indeed was the first night that I slept in quiet, and yet a scurvy dream would not suffer me to rest. For I was all the night troubled with a door which I could not get open, but at last I did it. With these phantasies I passed the time, till at length towards day I awaked.

The Fourth Day

I STILL lay in my bed and leisurely surveyed all the noble images and figures up and down about my chamber. On a sudden, I heard the music of coronets as if they had been already in procession. My page skipped out of the bed as if he had been at his wit's end and looked more like one dead than living. In what case I then was is easily imaginable: for he said the rest were already presented to the King. I knew not what else to do but weep outright and curse my own slothfulness, though I yet dressed myself. My page was ready long before me and ran out of the chamber to see how affairs might yet stand. He soon returned, and brought with him the joyful news that the time indeed was not yet passed but that I had only overslept my breakfast, they being unwilling to waken me because of my age, though now it was time for me to go with him to the fountain where the most part were assembled.

With this consolation my spirit returned again, wherefore I was soon ready with my habit and went after the page to the fountain in the aforementioned garden where I found that the lion, instead of his sword, had a pretty large tablet by him. Now having well viewed it, I found that it was taken out of the ancient monuments and placed here for some especial honour. The inscription was somewhat worn out with age, and therefore I am minded to set it down here, as it is, and give every one leave to consider it:

HERMES PRINCEPS.
POST TOT ILLATA
GENERI HUMANO DAMNA,
DEI CONSILIO:
ARTISQUE ADMINICULO,
MEDICINA SALUBRIS FACTUS
HEIC FLUO.
Bibat ex me qui potest: lavet, qui vult:
turbet qui audet:
BIBITE FRATRES, ET VIVITE.[1]

This writing might well be read and understood, and
may therefore fitly be here placed, because easier than
any of the rest. After we had first washed ourselves out

1 "Prince Hermes: After so many injuries committed by the human
race, having been made a healing medicine by God's counsel and the assistance of art: here I flow. Drink from me, who is able; wash who will; and
disturb who dares. Drink, brothers, and live!" The coded script has been
deciphered by Richard Kienast (*Johann Valentin und die vier echten Rosen-
kreutzer-Schriften* [Leipzig: Mayer & Müller, 1926], 68) as "1378," the year
ascribed to Christian Rosenkreutz's birth in the *Confessio*:

$$\infty = L = 50$$
$$> = C = 100$$
$$\circ: = C = 100$$
$$XX = 20$$
$$\circ IC = M = 1000$$
$$V/: = V = 5$$
$$vvv = III = 3$$
$$> = C = \underline{100}$$
$$1378$$

of the fountain and every man had taken a draught out of an entirely golden cup, we were once more again to follow the Virgin into the hall and there put on new apparel which was all of cloth of gold gloriously set out with flowers. There was also given to everyone another Golden Fleece which was set about with precious stones and various workmanship according to the utmost skill of each artificer. On it hung a weighty medal of gold whereon were figured the Sun and Moon in opposition; but on the other side stood this poesie: "The light of the Moon shall be as the light of the Sun, and the light of the Sun shall be seven times lighter than at present."[2] Our former jewels were laid in a little casket and committed to one of the waiters.

After this the Virgin led us out in our order, while the musicians waited ready at the door all appareled in red velvet with white guards. Thereupon a door (which I never saw open before) to the royal winding-stairs was unlocked. There the Virgin led us together with the music up three-hundred-sixty-five stairs. There we saw nothing but what was of extreme costly and artificial workmanship. The further we went, the more glorious still was the furniture, until at length at the top we came under a painted arch where the sixty virgins attended us, all richly appareled.

Now as soon as they had bowed to us (and we as well as we could had returned our reverence) our musicians were dispatched away and were fain to go down the winding-stairs again, the door being shut after them.

---

2 Isaiah 30:26.

After this a little bell was tolled whereat there came in a beautiful virgin who brought everyone a wreath of laurel, though our virgins had branches given them.

Meanwhile, a curtain was drawn up where I saw the King and Queen as they sat there in their Majesty. Had not the yesterday Queen so faithfully warned me, I should have forgotten myself and have equaled this unspeakable glory to Heaven: for, besides that the room glistered of pure gold and precious stones, the Queen's robes were moreover so made that I was not able to behold them. And whereas I before esteemed anything for handsome, here all things so much surpassed the rest as the stars in Heaven are elevated. In the meantime, the Virgin stepped in, with each of the virgins taking one of us by the hand, and with most profound reverence presented us to the King. Whereupon the Virgin began thus to speak:

"That to honour your Royal Majesties, most gracious King and Queen, these lords here present have adventured hither with peril of body and life. Your Majesties have reason to rejoice, especially since the greatest part are qualified for the enlarging of Your Majesties' estates and empire, as you will find the same by a most gracious and particular examination of each of them. Herewith I was desirous thus to have them in humility presented to your Majesties, with most humble suit to discharge me of this my commission and most graciously to take sufficient information from each of them concerning both my actions and omissions."

Hereupon she laid down her branch upon the ground. Now it would have been very fitting for one of us to have put in and spoken somewhat on this occasion, but seeing we were all troubled with the falling of the uvula.[3]

At length the old Atlas stepped forward and spoke on the King's behalf: "Their Royal Majesties do most graciously rejoice at your arrival and will that their Royal Grace be assured to all and every man. And with thy administration, gentle Virgin, they are most graciously satisfied, and accordingly a royal reward shall therefore be provided for thee. Yet it is still their intention that thou shalt this day also continue with them, in as much as they have no reason to mistrust thee."

Hereupon the Virgin humbly took up the branch again. And so we for this first time were to step aside with our Virgin. This room was square on the front, five times broader than it was long; but towards the west it had a great arch like a porch, wherein stood in circle three glorious royal thrones, the middlemost was somewhat higher than the rest. Now in each throne sat two persons. In the first sat a very ancient king with a gray beard, yet his consort was extraordinary fair and young. In the third throne sat a black king of middle age and by him a dainty old matron, not crowned but covered with a veil. But in the middle sat the two young persons, who, though they had likewise wreaths of laurel upon their heads, yet over them hung a large and costly crown. Now, albeit they were not at this time so fair as I had before imagined to myself, yet so it was to be. Behind them on a round form sat for the most part ancient men, yet none of them (at which I wondered) had any sword or other weapon about him; neither saw I

---

3 That is, "tongue-tied."

any other guards, but certain virgins which were with us the day before who sat on the sides of the arch.

Here can I not pass in silence how the little Cupid flew to and again there, but for the most part he hovered and played the wanton about the great crown.[4] Sometimes he seated himself in between the two lovers, somewhat smiling upon them with his bow. Nay, sometimes he made as if he would shoot one of us. In brief, this knave was so full of his waggery that he would not spare even the little birds, which in multitudes flew up and down the room, but tormented them all he could. The virgins also had their pastimes with him: but whensoever they could catch him, it was not so easy a matter for him to get away from them again. Thus this little knave made all the sport and mirth.

Before the Queen stood a small but unexpressibly curious altar wherein lay a book covered with black velvet only a little overlaid with gold. By this stood a small taper in an ivory candlestick, which, although it were very small, yet it burnt continually and stood in that manner that had not Cupid in sport now and then puffed upon it, we could not have conceived it to be fire. By this stood a sphere or celestial globe, which of itself turned clearly about. Next to this was a small striking-watch, and by that a little crystal pipe or syphon-fountain out of which perpetually ran a clear blood red liquor. Last of all was a skull, or death's head: in this

---

4 Another way of saying this is that Love (*Eros*) urges all things on to perfection, a notion expressed perhaps most famously in Plato's *Symposium*.

was a white serpent which was of such a length that, though she crept circle-wise about the rest of it, yet her tail still remained in one of the eye-holes until her head again entered at the other.[5] Thus she never stirred from her skull, unless it happened that Cupid twitched a little at her, for then she slipped in so suddenly that we all could not choose but marvel at it.

Together with this altar, there were up and down the room wonderful images which moved themselves as if they had been alive and had so strange a contrivance that it would be impossible for me to relate it all. Likewise, as we were passing out there began such a marvelous kind of vocal music that I could not certainly tell whether it were performed by the virgins who yet stayed behind or by the images themselves.

Now we, being for this time satisfied, went thence with our virgins, who, the musicians being already present, led us down the winding-stairs again; but the door was diligently locked and bolted as soon as we were come again into the hall. One of the virgins began, "I wonder sister, that you durst adventure yourself amongst so many persons."

"My sister," replied our President, "I am fearful of none so much as of this man"—pointing at me.

This speech went to the heart of me, for I well understood that she mocked at my age; and, indeed, I was the

---

5 Montgomery (*Cross and Crucible*, 2:397) notes that the English Paracelsian and Rosicrucian apologist Robert Fludd employs the skull and serpent motif for the title page of his *Tractatus theologo-philosophicus* (1617).

oldest of them all. Yet she comforted me again with promise that as long as I behaved myself well towards her she would easily rid me of this burden.

Meanwhile, a collation was again brought in, and by each one sat his virgin, who well knew how to shorten the time with handsome discourses. What their discourses and sports were I dare not blab out of school, but most of the questions were about the arts, whereby I could lightly gather that both young and old were conversant in the sciences. But still it ran in my thoughts how I might become young again, whereupon I was somewhat the sadder.

This the Virgin perceived and therefore began: "I dare lay anything that if I lie with him tonight, he shall be pleasanter in the morning." Hereupon they began to laugh, and albeit I blushed all over, yet I was fain to laugh too at my own misfortune.

There was one there that had a mind to return my disgrace again upon the Virgin, whereupon he said, "I hope not only we, but the virgins themselves will bear witness in behalf of our brother that our Lady President hath promised herself to be his bedfellow tonight."

"I should be well content with it," replied the Virgin, "if I had not reason to be afraid of these my sisters: there would be no hold with them should I choose the best and handsomest for myself against their will."

"My sister," presently began another, "we find hereby that thy high office makes thee not proud; wherefore, if by thy permission we might by lot part the lords here present amongst us for bedfellows, thou shouldst with our goodwill have such a prerogative."

We let this pass thus for a jest and began again to discourse together. But our Virgin could not leave tormenting us and therefore began again:

"My lords, how if we should permit Fortune to decide which of us must lie together tonight?"

"Well," said I, "if it may be no otherwise, we cannot refuse such a proffer."

Now because it was concluded to make this trial, after the meal we resolved to sit no longer at table; so we arose and each one walked up and down with his virgin.

"Nay," said the Virgin, "it shall not be so yet, but let us see how Fortune will couple us" upon which we were separated asunder.

But now first arose a dispute how the business should be carried, but this was only a premeditated device, for the Virgin instantly made the proposal that we should mix ourselves together in a ring, and that she beginning to count from herself, the seventh, was to be content with the following seventh, whether it were a Virgin or man. For our parts, we were not aware of any craft, and therefore permitted it so to be. But when we thought we had very well mingled ourselves, the virgins nevertheless were so subtle that each one knew her station beforehand. The Virgin began to reckon, the seventh next her was again a virgin, the third seventh a virgin likewise, and this happened so long till (to our amazement) all the virgins came forth and none of us was hit. Thus we poor pitiful wretches remained standing alone, and were moreover forced to suffer ourselves to be jeered, too, and confess we were very handsomely cozened. In short, whoever had seen us in our order might sooner have expected the sky to fall than that it should never have come to our turn. Herewith our sport was at an end, and we were fain to satisfy ourselves with the Virgin's waggery.[6]

In the interim, the little wanton Cupid came also in unto us. But because he presented himself on behalf of their Royal Majesties and delivered us a health (as from them) out of a golden cup and was to call our virgins to the King, withal declaring he could at this time tarry no longer with them, we could not sufficiently sport ourselves with him. So, with a due return of our most humble thanks, we let him fly forth again. Now, because (in the interim) the mirth began to fall into my consort's feet and the virgins were nothing sorry to see it, they quickly led up a civil dance, which I rather beheld with pleasure than assisted. My Mercurialists[7] were, indeed, so ready with their postures as if they had been long of the trade. After some few dances our President came in again and told us how the artists and students had offered themselves to their Royal Majesties for their honour and pleasure before their departure to act a merry comedy; and said it would be acceptable to them that, if we thought good to be present at it, we might wait upon their Royal Majesties to the House of the Sun and they would most graciously acknowledge it. Hereupon we at once returned our most humble thanks for the honour vouchsafed us; not only that, but we moreover most submissively tendered our small service.

This the Virgin related again and presently brought

6 *Eros* here leads each one along in the work while ensuring the chastity of all involved. One of the beneficial uses of *eros*.

7 Alchemists as "sons of Hermes" (Mercury).

word to attend their Royal Majesties (in our order) in the gallery. Thither we were soon led, though we stayed not long there, for the Royal Procession was just ready (yet without any music at all). The unknown queen who was yesterday with us went foremost appareled in white satin with a small and costly coronet. She carried nothing but a small crucifix which was made of a pearl, and this very day wrought between the young King and his Bride. After her went the six aforementioned virgins in two ranks who carried the King's jewels belonging to the little altar. Next to these came the three Kings. The Bridegroom was in the midst of them in a plain dress: only in black satin after the Italian mode. He had on a small round black hat with a little black pointed feather which he courteously put off to us, thereby to signify his favour towards us. To him we bowed ourselves, as also to the first, as we had been before instructed. After the kings came the three queens, two whereof were richly habited. She in the middle went likewise all in black, and Cupid held up her train. After this, intimation was given to us to follow, and after us the virgins, till at last old Atlas brought up the rear.

In such procession, through many stately walks we at length came to the House of the Sun, placed next to the King and Queen upon a richly furnished scaffold, to behold the fore-ordained comedy. We, indeed, though separated, stood on the right hand of the kings, but the virgins on the left, except those to whom the royal ensigns were committed. To them was allotted a peculiar standing at top of all. But the rest of the attendants were fain to stand below between the columns, and therewith to be content.

Now because there are many remarkable passages in this comedy, I will not omit in brief to run it over:

First of all came forth a very ancient king with some servants. Before his throne was brought a little chest, with mention that it was found upon the water. Now, it being opened, there appeared in it a lovely babe together with certain jewels and a small letter of parchment sealed and superscribed to the king.[8] The King therefore presently opened the parchment and, having read it, wept. He then declared to his servants how injuriously the King of the Moors had deprived his aunt of her country, and had extinguished all the royal seed even to this infant. With the daughter of that country he had now purposed to have matched his son. Hereupon he swore to maintain perpetual enmity with the Moor and his allies to revenge this upon him. Therewith he commanded that the child should be tenderly nursed, and to that they should make preparation against the Moor. Now this provision and the discipline of the young lady (who after she was a little grown up was committed to an ancient tutor) continued all the first act with many very fine and laudable sports besides.

In the interlude, a lion and griffin were set at one

---

8 Note the similarity to the story of Moses. In Shakespeare's *Pericles* the infant Marina with her mother Thaissa is likewise placed into a chest. On the alchemical connotations of this play, see Lyndy Abraham's "Weddings, Funerals, and Incest: Alchemical Emblems and Shakespeare's *Pericles, Prince of Tyre*," *The Journal of English and Germanic Philology* 98 no. 4 (Oct. 1999): 523–49.

another to fight; and the lion got the victory, which was also a pretty fight.[9]

In the second act, the Moor, a very black treacherous fellow, came forth also. He, having with vexation understood that his murder was discovered—and that, too, a little lady was craftily stolen from him—began thereupon to consult how by stratagem he might be able to encounter so powerful an adversary. He was then at length advised by certain fugitives who by reason of famine fled to him. The young lady, contrary to all men's expectation, fell again into his hands. She, had he not been wonderfully deceived by his own servants, had like to have been slain. Thus this act too was concluded with a marvelous triumph of the Moor.

In the third act a great army on the King's party was raised against the Moor and put under the conduct of an ancient and valiant knight who fell into the Moor's country. At length he forcibly rescued the young lady out of the tower and appareled her anew. After this, in a trice they erected a glorious scaffold and placed their young lady upon it. Presently came twelve royal ambassadors, amongst whom the aforementioned knight made a speech alleging that the King his most gracious lord had not only heretofore delivered her from death, and even hitherto caused her to be royally brought up (though she had not behaved herself altogether as became her), but, moreover, his Royal Majesty had

9 "The fighting lion and griffin represent the simultaneous dissolution (*separatio*) and coagulation (*coniunctio*) of the matter of the Stone at an early stage of the opus" (Lyndy Abraham, *Dictionary of Alchemical Imagery*, 94).

before others elected her to be a spouse for the young lord his son. He furthermore most graciously desired that the said espousals might be really executed in case they would be sworn to His Majesty upon the following articles. Hereupon, out of a parchment he caused certain glorious conditions to be read, which, if it were not too long, were well worthy to be here recounted. In brief, the young lady took an oath inviolably to observe the same, returning thanks withal in most seemly sort for this so high a grace. At this they began to sing to the praise of God, of the King, and the young lady; and so for this time departed.

For sport, in the meanwhile, the four beasts of Daniel, as he saw them in the vision and hath at large described them, were brought in: all which had its certain signification.

In the fourth act, the young lady was again restored to her lost kingdom and crowned, and was for a space in this array conducted about the place with extraordinary joy. After this, many and various ambassadors presented themselves, not only to wish her prosperity, but also to behold her glory. Yet it was not long that she preserved her integrity, but soon began again to look wantonly about her and to wink at the ambassadors and lords, wherein she truly acted her part to the life.

These her manners were soon known to the Moor, who would by no means neglect such an opportunity. Because her steward had not sufficient regard to her, she was easily blinded with great promises so that she had no good confidence in her King but privily submitted herself to the entire disposal of the Moor. Hereupon the Moor made haste and, having (by her consent) got-

ten her into his hands, he gave her good words so long
till all her kingdom had subjected itself to him. Then, in
the third scene of this act, he caused her to be led forth
and first to be stripped stark naked and upon a scurvy
wooden scaffold to be bound to a post and well
scourged, and at last sentenced to death. This was so
woeful a spectacle that it made the eyes of many to run
over. Naked as she was, she was cast into prison, there
to expect her death, which was to be procured by poi-
son, which yet killed her not, but made her leprous all
over. Thus this act was for the most part lamentable.

Between acts, they brought forth Nebuchadnezzar's
image, which was adorned with all manner of arms: on
the head, breast, belly, legs, and feet, and the like. Of
this more shall be spoken in the future explication.

In the fifth act the young king was acquainted with all
that had passed between the Moor and his future
spouse. The young king first interceded with his father
for her, entreating that she might not be left in that condition. Having agreed to this, ambassadors were dispatched to comfort her in her sickness and captivity, but
yet withal to give her notice of her inconsideratedness.
She would not yet receive them, but consented to be the
Moor's concubine, which was also done, and the young
king was acquainted with it.

After this act came a band of fools, each of which
brought with him a cudgel wherewith in a trice they
made a great globe of the world, and as soon undid it
again. It was a fine sportive phantasy.

In the sixth act, the young king resolved to bid battle
to the Moor, which also was done. Albeit the Moore was
discomfited, yet all held the young king for dead. At

length he came to himself again, released his spouse, and committed her to his steward and chaplain. The first of these tormented her mightily until at last the leaf turned over; and the priest was so insolently wicked that he would needs be above all. This was reported to the young king, who hastily dispatched one who broke the neck of the priest's mightiness[10] and adorned the bride in some measure for the nuptials.

After the act a vast artificial elephant was brought forth. He carried a great tower with musicians, which was also well-pleasing to all.

In the last act the Bridegroom appeared in such pomp as is not well to be believed, and I was amazed how it was brought to pass. The Bride met him in the like solemnity, whereupon all the people cried out "*VIVAT SPONSUS! VIVAT SPONSA!*"[11] And by this comedy they did with all congratulate our King and Queen in the most stately manner. This (as I well observed) pleased them most extraordinary well.

At length they made some passes about the stage in such procession, till at last they altogether began thus to sing:

I

This time full of love
Does our joy much improve
Because of the King's nuptial;
And therefore let's sing
That from all parts 't may ring,
Blest be he that granted us all.

10 Montgomery, ever the stalwart Lutheran, reads Martin Luther himself here. See *Cross and Crucible*, 2:409.

11 "Long live the Bridegroom! Long live the Bride!"

II

The Bride most exquisitely fair,
Whom we attended with long care,
To him in troth's now plighted:
We fully have at length obtain'd,
The same for which we did contend:
He's happy that's fore-sighted.

III

Now the parents kind and good
By entreaties are subdu'd:
Long enough in hold was she mew'd;
In honour increase,
Till thousands arise.
And spring from your own proper blood.

After this, thanks were returned and the comedy was finished with joy to the particular good liking of the Royal Persons, wherefore, the evening also being already hard by, all departed together in their aforementioned order. We were then to attend the Royal Persons up the winding-stairs into the hall (where the tables were already richly furnished) and this was the first time that we were invited to the King's table. The little altar was placed in the midst of the hall and the six forenamed royal ensigns were laid on it. At this time, the young King behaved himself very graciously towards us, but yet he could not be heartily merry; and although he now and then discoursed a little with us, yet he often sighed, at which the little Cupid only mocked and played his waggish tricks.

The old King and Queen were very serious, and only the wife of one of the ancient kings was gay enough, the cause whereof I yet understood not. During this, the Royal Persons took up the first table, while at the second we only sat. At the third, some of the principal virgins placed themselves. The rest of the virgins and men were all fain to wait. This was performed with such state and solemn stillness that I am afraid to make many words of it. Here, I cannot leave untouched how that all the Royal Persons, before meat, attired themselves in snow-white, glittering garments, and so sat down to table. Over the table hung the aforementioned great golden crown, the precious stones, which, without any other light, would have sufficiently illuminated the hall. However, all the lights were kindled at the small taper upon the altar: what the reason was I did not certainly know. But this I took very good notice of: that the young King frequently sent meat to the white serpent upon the little altar. This caused me to muse. Almost all the prattle at this banquet was made by little Cupid, who could not leave us (and me especially) untormented. He was perpetually producing some strange matter. However, there was no considerable mirth: all went silently on. From this I, by myself, could imagine some great imminent peril. There was no music at all heard, but if we were demanded anything we were fain to give short, round answers, and so let it rest. In short, all things had so strange a face that the sweat began to trickle down all over my body;[12] and I am apt to believe that the stout-heartedest man alive would then have lost his courage.

12 One interpretation might be that the chemical transformation, symbolized in all that is happening around him, is actually taking place within CRC himself.

Supper being now almost ended, the young King commanded the book to be reached him from the little altar. This he opened and caused it once again by an old man to be propounded to us, whether we resolved to abide with him in prosperity and adversity. We, having with trembling consented to this, he further caused us sadly to be demanded whether we would give him our hands on it, which, when we could find no evasion, was fain so to be. Hereupon one after another arose and with his own hand writ himself down in this book. When this also was performed, the little crystal fountain together with a very small crystal glass was brought near, out of which all the Royal Persons one after another drank. Afterwards it was reached to us, too, and so forward to all persons. This was called the *Haustus Silentii*.[13] Hereupon all the Royal Persons presented us their hands, declaring that in case we did not now stick to them, we should now and never more hereafter see them, which verily made our eyes run over. But our President engaged herself and promised very largely on our behalf, which gave them satisfaction.

In the meantime, a little bell was tolled, at which all the Royal Persons waxed so mighty bleak that we were ready utterly to despair. They quickly put off their white garments again and put on entirely black ones. The whole hall likewise was hung about with black velvet. The floor was also covered with black velvet, with which also the ceiling above (all this being before pre-

---

13 "Draught of Silence."

pared) was overspread.[14] After that the tables were also removed away and all had seated themselves round about upon the form. We also had put on black habits. In came our President again (who was before gone out) and brought with her six black taffeta scarves with which she bound the six Royal Persons' eyes. Now, when they could no longer see, there were immediately brought in by the servants six covered coffins and set down in the hall, and also a low black seat placed in the midst. Finally, there stepped in a very coal-black, tall man who bare in his hand a sharp axe.

After that, the old King had been first brought to the seat. His head was instantly whipped off and wrapped up in a black cloth, but the blood was received into a great golden goblet and placed with him in the coffin that stood by, which, being covered, was set aside. Thus it went with the rest also, so that I thought it would at length have come to me, too, but it did not. For as soon as the six Royal Persons were beheaded, the black man went out again, after whom another followed, who beheaded him, too, just before the door, and brought back his head together with the axe, which were laid in a little chest.

14 The color black in alchemy represents the *nigredo*, the stage or stages of putrefaction, the complete destruction of *materia* in order to disclose the *prima materia*. White represents the *albedo* stage or albification, a stage of perfection in the work. Andreae seems to be suggesting here that even though the royal couples of the story have a marked degree of nobility (as in the "noble metals" of silver and gold) they still have not achieved the Philosopher's Stone. The change from white to black further suggests that the royal couples are at the silver stage of transmutation, the penultimate stage to "gold-making," the completion of the Work.

This, indeed, to me seemed a bloody bedding, but, because I could not tell what would yet be the event, I was fain for that time to captivate my understanding until I were further resolved. For the Virgin, too, seeing that some of us were faint-hearted and wept, bid us be content. For, said she to us, the life of these standeth now in your hands; and, if you follow me, this death shall make many alive. Herewith she intimated we should go sleep and trouble ourselves no further on our part, for they should be sure to have their due right. And so she bade us all good night, saying that she must watch the dead bodies this night. We did so, and were each of us conducted by our pages into our lodgings. My page talked with me of sundry and various matters (which I still very well remember) and gave me cause enough to admire at his understanding. But his intention was to lull me asleep, which at last I well observed, whereupon I made as though I were fast asleep, but no sleep came into my eyes: I could not put the beheaded out of my mind.

Now, my lodging was directly over against the great lake, so that I could well look upon it, the windows being nigh the bed. About midnight, as soon as it had struck twelve, on a sudden I espied on the lake a great fire, wherefore out of fear I quickly opened the window to see what would become of it. From afar I saw seven ships making forward which were all stuck full of lights. Above on the top of each of them hovered a flame that passed to and fro and sometimes descended quite down, so that I could lightly judge that it must needs be the spirits of the beheaded. These ships gently approached to land and each of them had no more than one mariner.

As soon as they were now gotten to shore, I presently espied our Virgin with a torch going towards the ships, after whom the six covered coffins together with the little chest were carried, each of them privily laid in a ship.

At this, I awaked my page, too, who hugely thanked me: for having run much up and down all the day, he might quite have overslept this, though he well knew it. As soon as the coffins were laid in the ships, all the lights were extinguished and the six flames passed back together over the lake, so that there was no more but one light in each ship for a watch. There were also some hundreds of watchmen who had encamped themselves on the shore and sent the Virgin back again into the castle, which she carefully bolted all up again. I could well judge that there was nothing more to be done this night, but that we must expect the day; so we again betook ourselves to rest. I only of all my company had a chamber towards the lake and saw this. Now I was also extreme weary, and so fell asleep in my manifold speculations.

The Fifth Day[1]

HE night was over and the dear wished-for day broken when I got me out of the bed, more desirous to learn what might yet ensue now that I had sufficiently slept. After I had put on my clothes and, according to my custom, was gone down the stairs, it was still too early. I found nobody else in the hall, wherefore I entreated my page to lead me a little about in the castle and shew me somewhat that was rare. He was now (as always) willing and presently led me down certain steps underground to a great iron door, upon which the following words in great copper letters were fixed:

---

1 Thomas Willard recognizes a symmetry in the structure in the *CW* in the way the last three days mirror the first three: "On the last Christian returns home, on the penultimate he ascends the seven levels of an alchemical tower where the chemical wedding takes place, and on the day before that he faces a personal test before traveling to the tower. At the end of each day, he has a dream or vision." See his "Dreams and Symbols in *The Chemical Wedding*," 137.

This I thus copied and set down in my table-book.[2] After this door was opened, the page led me by the hand through a very dark passage till we came again to a very little door that was now only put to; for (as the page informed me) it was first opened but yesterday, when the coffins were taken out, and had not been since shut. As soon as we stepped in, I espied the most precious thing that Nature ever created: for this vault had no other light but from certain huge great carbuncles. This (as I was informed) was the King's treasury. But the most glorious and principal thing that I here saw was a sepulcher (which stood in the middle) so rich that I wondered it was no better guarded. At this the page answered me that I had good reason to be thankful to my planet, by whose influence it was that I had now seen certain pieces which no human eye else (except the King's family) had ever had a view of.

This sepulcher was triangular and had in the middle of it a kettle of polished copper; the rest was of pure gold and precious stones. In the kettle stood an angel who held in his arms an unknown tree from which fruits continually dropped into the kettle; and as oft as the fruit fell into the kettle, it turned into water and ran

---

2 The cipher, so mysterious and occult (at first glance), was discovered by Nicolaus Seeländer in *Hamburgischen Berichte von Gelehrten Sachen*, No. 39, 343–47; No. 97, 874–77 (1736) and reads as follows: *Hye lygt begraben / VENUS / dye schön Fraw, so manchen / Hoen man / umb glück, her, segen, und wolfart / gebracht hatt*. Translated into English: "Here lies buried VENUS, the beautiful woman who so many great men has robbed of fortune, honor, blessing, and prosperity." The code is, of course, divulged by the page straightaway—though he never lets on that he has decoded it. Another of Andreae's tricks.

out from thence into three small golden kettles standing by. This little altar was supported by these three animals: an Eagle, an Ox, and a Lion, which stood on an exceeding costly base. I asked my page what this might signify. "Here," said he, "lies buried Lady Venus, that beauty which hath undone many a great man in fortune, honour, blessing, and prosperity." After this he shewed me a copper door on the pavement. "Here," said he, "if you please, we may go further down." "I still follow you," replied I. So I went down the steps, where it was exceeding dark, but the page immediately opened a little chest wherein stood a small ever-burning taper at which he kindled one of the many torches which lay by. I was mightily terrified, and seriously asked how he durst do this? He gave me for answer: "As long as the Royal Persons are still at rest, I have nothing to fear."

Herewith I espied a rich bed readymade and hung about with curious curtains, one of which he drew, where I saw the Lady Venus[3] stark naked (for he heaved up the coverlets, too) lying there in such beauty and in a fashion so surprising that I was almost beside myself.

---

3 Both Pierre Hadot and Mary Midgley discuss the idea of Isis veiled (and unveiled) in early modern philosophy and natural science. For Hadot, this presaged the race for power that has characterized the sciences since the scientific revolution. For Midgley, this resulted in an ethos equivalent to rape culture: where nature is seen as a phenomenon to be unveiled, explored, and forced into compulsion. As Hadot points out, perhaps only Goethe (as a scientist) took a stand against this underlying psychic disorder that has plagued the sciences ever since. See Pierre Hadot, *The Veil of Isis: An Essay on the History of the Idea of Nature*, trans. Michael Chase (Cambridge: The Belknap Press of Harvard University Press, 2006); Mary Midgley, *Science as Salvation: A Modern Myth and Its Meaning* (London: Routledge, 1992), especially pp. 77–78.

Neither do I yet know whether it was a piece thus carved or a human corpse that lay dead there, for she was altogether immoveable—and yet I durst not touch her. She was again covered and the curtain drawn before her, yet she was still (as it were) in my eye. But I soon espied behind the bed a tablet, upon which it was thus written:[4]

I asked my page concerning this writing, but he laughed, with the promise that I should know it, too. So,

he putting out the torch, we again ascended. Then I better viewed all the little doors and first found that on every corner there burned a small taper of pyrites, of which I had before taken no notice: for the fire was so

---

4 *Wan dye Frucht meynes / baums wyrt vollends / verschmelzen, werde ych / aufwachen und eyn / muter syn eynes / Konygs.* "When the fruit of my tree melts, I will awaken and be the mother of a king." The page, of course, spills the beans of this "secret" as well.

clear that it looked much more like a stone than a taper. From this heat the tree was forced continually to melt, yet it still produced new fruit. "Now behold," said the page, "what I heard revealed to the King by Atlas: when the tree (said he) shall be quite melted down then shall Lady Venus awake and be the mother of a king."

Whilst he was thus speaking, in flew the little Cupid, who at first was somewhat abashed at our presence, but seeing us both look more like the dead than the living, he could not at length refrain from laughing. He demanded what spirit had brought me thither, and I with trembling answered that I had lost my way in the castle and was by chance come hither, and that the page likewise had been looking up and down for me and had at last lighted upon me here. I hoped he would not take it amiss. "Nay, then, 'tis well enough," said Cupid "my old busy grandsire—but you might lightly have served me a scurvy trick had you been aware of this door. Now I must look better to it." At this he put a strong lock on the copper door where we before had descended.

I thanked God that he lighted upon us no sooner. My page, too, was the more jocund because I had so well helped him at this pinch. "Yet, can I not," said Cupid, "let it pass unrevenged that you were so near stumbling upon my dear mother." With that he put the point of his dart into one of the little tapers and, heating it a little, pricked me with it on the hand. At that time I little regarded it, but was glad that it went so well with us and that we came off without further danger.

Meanwhile, my companions were gotten out of bed and were again returned into the hall. To them I also joined myself, making as if I were then first risen. After

Cupid had carefully made all fast again, he came like-wise to us and would needs have me shew him my hand. There he still found a little drop of blood, at which he heartily laughed and bade the rest have a care of me— for I would shortly end my days. We all wondered how Cupid could be so merry and have no sense at all of the yesterday's sad passages. But he was no whit troubled.

Our President had in the meantime made herself ready for the journey, coming in all in black velvet, yet she still bare her branch of laurel. Her virgins, too, had their branches. All things now being in readiness, the Virgin bade us first drink somewhat and then presently prepare for the procession. We made no long tarrying, but followed her out of the hall into the court.

In the court stood six coffins. My companions thought no other but that the six Royal Persons lay in them, but I well observed the device. Yet, I knew not what was to be done with these other. By each coffin were eight muffled men, and as soon as the music went (it was so mournful and dolesome a tune that I was astonished at it) they took up the coffins and we (as we were ordered) were fain to go after them into the gar-den. In the midst of the garden was erected a wooden edifice having round about the roof a glorious crown and standing upon seven columns.

Within the building were formed six sepulchers, and by each of them a stone; but in the middle it had a round, hollow rising stone. In these graves the coffins were quietly and with many ceremonies laid. The stones were shoved over them, and they were shut fast. But the little chest was to lie in the middle. By this were my companions deceived, for they imagined no other but that the corpses of the dead were there. Upon the top of all there was a great flag, having a phoenix painted on it, perhaps therewith the more to delude us.[5] Here I had great occasion to thank God that I had seen more than the rest.

After the funerals were done, the Virgin, having placed herself upon the middlemost stone, made a short oration that we should be constant to our engagements and not repine at the pains we were hereafter to undergo, but that we should be helpful in restoring the present buried Royal Persons to life again, and therefore without delay to rise up with her to make a journey to the Tower of Olympus to fetch from thence medicines useful and necessary for this purpose. This we soon agreed to and followed her through another little door quite to the shore. There the seven ships stood all empty, in which all the virgins stuck up their laurel branches. After they had distributed us in the six ships, they caused us in God's name thus to begin our voyage and looked upon us as long as they could have us in sight. After this they with all the watchmen returned into the castle.

Our ships had each of them a peculiar device. Five of them, indeed, had the five *Corporus Regularia*,[6] each a several one, but mine (in which the Virgin, too, sat) carried a globe. Thus we sailed on in a singular order, and each had only two mariners.

5 The phoenix represents both resurrection and the achievement of the Philosopher's Stone.

6. The "regular bodies" are the three-dimensional geometric shapes known also as the platonic solids. They have equal sides and angles and

a

||

b|| c|| d|

e|| f||

g||

Foremost went the ship (*a*), in which, as I conceive, the Moor lay. In this were twelve musicians who played excellent well. Its device was a pyramid.[7] Next followed three abreast (*b*, *c*, and *d*) in which we were disposed. I sat in *c*. In the midst behind these came the two fairest and stateliest ships (*e* and *f*) stuck about with many branches of laurel, having no passengers in them. Their flags were the Sun and Moon.[8] But in the rear was only one ship (*g*), and in this were forty virgins.

Being thus passed over this lake, we first came through a narrow arm into the right sea, where all the sirens, nymphs, and sea-goddesses attended us. They immediately dispatched a sea-nymph to us to deliver their present and offering of honour to the wedding. It was a

---

only five of them exist: the tetrahedron (4 sides), octahedron (8 sides), dodecahedron (12 sides), icosahedron (20 sides) and cube or hexahedron (6 sides). Plato discusses their cosmological significance in the *Timaeus*. Johannes Kepler, in *Mysterium Cosmographicum* (1596), provides an elegant model of the cosmos based on an idea of the platonic solids nested inside one another, which he believed corresponded to the orbits of the planets relative to one another. Though he would later discover the elliptical orbits of the planets (anticipating the theory of gravity), his platonic version was not as inexact as one might think. From antiquity, the platonic solids also have had correspondences with the elements: the tetrahedron with fire, the octahedron with air, the icosahedron with water, the cube with earth, and the dodecahedron with ether.

7 That is, the tetrahedron.

8 The Sun and Moon (*Sol* and *Luna*) of alchemy are "the Royal Pair" and correspond, among other things, to the King and Queen, gold and silver, male and female, the Bridegroom and the Bride.

costly, great, set, round, and orient pearl, the like to which hath not at any time been seen, either in ours or yet in the New World. The Virgin having friendly received it, the nymph further entreated that audience might be given to their divertissements and to make a little stand. This the Virgin was content to do and she then commanded the two great ships to stand into the middle and with the rest to encompass them in pentagon. After this the nymphs fell into a ring about them and with a most delicate sweet voice began thus to sing:[9]

I

There's nothing better here below
Than beauteous, noble Love;
Whereby we like to God do grow,
And none to grief do move.

---

9 The song may also serve as a commentary on the activities of Cupid/ Eros in the narrative. Ioan Couliano, in his groundbreaking text *Eros and Magic in the Renaissance*, argues that eros was as essential to the scientific understanding of the Renaissance as mechanical laws of physics are today. Citing Giordano Bruno's *De vinculis in genere* (16th c.), Couliano describes the importance of the imagination of Eros during the period: "Eros 'is lord of the world: he pushes, directs, controls and appeases everyone. All other bonds are reduced to that one, as we see in the animal kingdom where no female and no male tolerates rivals, even forgetting to eat and drink, even at the risk of life itself.' In conclusion, *vinculum quippe vinculorum amor est*, 'indeed, the chain of chains is love.'" See Ioan P. Couliano, *Eros and Magic in the Renaissance*, trans. Margaret Cook (Chicago: University of Chicago Press, 1983), 97.

Wherefore let's chant it to the King,
That all the sea thereof may ring.
We question; answer you.

II

What was it that at first us made?
    'Twas Love.
And what hath grace afresh convey'd?
    'Tis Love.
Whence was't (pray tell us) we were born?
    Of Love
How came we then again forlorn?
    Sans Love.

III

Who was it (say) that us conceiv'd?
    'Twas Love.
Who suckled, nursed, and reliev'd?
    'Twas Love.
What is it we to our parents owe?
    'Tis Love.
Why do they us such kindness show?
    Of Love.

IV

Who gets herein the victory?
    'Tis Love.
Can Love by search obtained be?
    By Love.
How may a man good works perform?
    Through Love.
Who into one can two transform?
    'Tis Love.

V

Then let our song sound,
Till its echo rebound.
To Love's honour and praise,
Which may ever increase
With our noble princes, the King and the Queen,
The soul is departed, their bodies within.

VI

And as long as we live,
God graciously give;
That as great Love and Amity,
They bear each other mightily:
So we likewise, by Love's own Flame,
May reconjoin them once again.

VII

Then this annoy
Into great joy
(If many thousand younglings deign)
Shall change, and ever so remain.

They, having with most admirable conceit and melody finished this song, I no more wondered at Ulysses for stopping the ears of his companions: for I seemed to myself the most unhappy man alive that Nature had not made me, too, so trim a creature. But the Virgin soon dispatched them and commanded to set sail from thence. At this the nymphs, too, after they had been presented with a long red scarf for a gratuity, went off and dispersed themselves in the sea.

I was at this time sensible that Cupid began to work with me, too, which yet tended but very little to my credit; and, for as much as my giddiness is likely to be nothing beneficial to the reader, I am resolved to let it rest as it is. This was the very wound that in the first book I received on the head in a dream: and let everyone take warning by me of loitering about Venus's bed—for Cupid can by no means brook it.

After some hours, having in friendly discourses made a good way, we came within ken of the Tower of Olympus, wherefore the Virgin commanded by the discharge of some pieces to give the signal of our approach, which was also done. Immediately we espied a great white flag thrust out and a small gilded pinnace sent forth to meet us. As soon as this was come to us, we perceived in it a very ancient man, the Warden of the Tower, with certain guards clothed in white, of whom we were friendly received and so conducted to the Tower.

This Tower was situated upon an island exactly square which was environed with a wall so firm and thick that I myself counted two-hundred-and-sixty passes over.[10] On the other side of the wall was a fine meadow with certain little gardens in which grew strange (and to me unknown) fruits, and then again an inner wall round about the Tower. The Tower itself was just as if seven round towers had been built one by another, yet the middlemost was somewhat the higher and within they all entered one into another, and had seven stories one above another. Being thus come to the gates of the Tower, we were led a little aside on the wall,

---

10 Kienast (85) identifies this number as a printer's error for 360; an assessment with which Montgomery concurs (*Cross and Crucible*, 2:433). There is certainly much to commend such an argument.

that so, as I well observed, the coffins might be brought into the Tower without our taking notice. Of this the rest knew nothing.

This being done, we were conducted into the Tower at the very bottom, which, albeit it were excellently painted, yet we had here little recreation: for this was nothing but a laboratory where we were fain to beat and wash plants, precious stones, and all sorts of things, extract their juice and essence, and put up the same in glasses—and then deliver them to be laid up. And, truly, our Virgin was so busy with us and so full of her directions, that she knew how to give each of us employment enough so that in this island we were fain to be mere drudges till we had achieved all that was necessary for the restoring of the beheaded bodies.

In the meantime (as I afterwards understood) three virgins were in the first apartment washing the corpses with all diligence. Having at length almost done with this our preparation, nothing more was brought us but some broth with a little draught of wine—whereby I well observed that we were not here for our pleasure.[11] Indeed, for when we had finished our day's work, everyone had only a mattress laid on the ground for him wherewith we were to content ourselves.

For my part I was not very much troubled with sleep, and therefore walked out into the garden, at length coming as far as the wall. Because the heaven was at that time very clear, I could well drive away the time in con-

11 The work of the alchemist, that is, is a work of asceticism not unlike that undertaken by those under the religious vows of poverty, obedience, and chastity.

templating the stars. By chance I came to a great pair of stone stairs which led up to the top of the wall. And because the moon shone very bright, I was so much the more confident and went up and looked too a little upon the sea, which was now exceeding calm. Thus, having good opportunity to consider better of astronomy, I found that this present night there would happen such a conjunction of the planets the like to which was not otherwise suddenly to be observed.

Having looked a good while into the sea (and it being just about midnight) as soon as it had struck twelve I beheld from far the seven flames passing over sea hitherward and betaking themselves to the top of the spire of the Tower. This made me somewhat afraid: for, as soon as the flames had settled themselves, the winds arose and began to make the sea very tempestuous. The moon also was covered with clouds, and my joy ended with such fear that I had scarce time enough to hit upon the stairs again and betake myself again to the Tower. Whether the flames tarried any longer or passed away again I cannot say: for in this obscurity I durst no more venture abroad. Therefore, I laid me down upon my mattress and, there being besides in the laboratory a pleasant and gently purling fountain, I fell asleep so much the sooner. And thus this fifth day, too, was concluded with wonders.

The Sixth Day

THE next morning, after we had awaked one another, we sat together awhile to discourse what might yet be the event of things. Some were of the opinion that they should all be enlivened again together. Others contradicted it because the decease of the ancients was not only to restore life, but increase, too, to the young ones. Some imagined that they were not put to death, but that others were beheaded in their stead.

We having now talked together a pretty while, the old man came in to us and, first saluting us, looked about him to see if all things were ready and the processes enough done. We had herein so behaved ourselves that he had no fault to find with our diligence, whereupon he placed all the glasses together and put them into a case. Presently came certain youths bringing with them some ladders, ropes, and large wings which they laid down before us and then departed. Then the old man began thus:

"My dear sons, one of these three things must each of you this day constantly bear about with him. It is free for you either to make a choice of one of them, or to cast lots about it." We replied that we would choose. "Nay," said he, "let it rather go by lot."

Hereupon he made three little schedules: in one he writ "Ladder," on the second "Rope," and on the third "Wings."[1] These he laid in a hat, and each man must

1. Bleiler suggests these may represent three different types of alche-

draw, and whatever he happened upon, that was to be his. Those who got the ropes imagined themselves to be in the best case; but I chanced on a ladder, which hugely afflicted me, for it was twelve-foot long and pretty weighty and I must be forced to carry it, whereas the others could handsomely coil their ropes about them. As for the wings, the old man joined them so neatly on to the third sort as if they had grown upon them.

At this he turned the cock and then the fountain ran no longer; we were fain to remove it from the middle out of the way. After all things were carried off, he, taking with him the casket with the glasses, took leave and locked the door fast after him so that we imagined no other but that we had been imprisoned in this Tower. But it was hardly a quarter of an hour before a round hole at the very top was uncovered, where we saw our Virgin. She called to us and bade us good morrow, desiring us to come up. They with the wings were instantly above through the hole. Only they with the ropes were in evil plight: for as soon as ever one of us was up, he was commanded to draw up the ladder to him. At last each man's rope was hanged on an iron hook, so everyone was fain to climb up by his rope as well as he could, which indeed was not compassed without blisters.

As soon as we were all well up, the hole was again covered and we were friendly received by the Virgin. This room was the whole breadth of the Tower itself, having six very stately vestries a little raised above the

my, two chemical (represented by ladders and ropes) and one spiritual (wings). See his "Johann Valentin Andreae, Fantasist and Utopist," 14.

room to be entered by the ascent of three steps. In these vestries we were distributed, there to pray for the life of the King and Queen. Meanwhile, the Virgin went in and out at the little door till we had done.

As soon as our process was absolved, there was brought in and placed in the middle through the little door by twelve persons (which were formerly our musicians) a wonderful thing of a longish shape, which my companions took only to be a fountain. But I well observed that the corpses lay in it: for the inner chest was of an oval figure, so large that six persons might well lie in it one by another. After this they again went forth, fetched their instruments, and conducted with our Virgin together with her she-attendants a most delicate noise of music.

The Virgin carried a little casket, but the rest only branches and small lamps, and some, too, lighted torches. The torches were immediately given into our hands, and we were to stand about the fountain in this order:

First stood the Virgin (*A*) with her attendants in a ring round about with the lamps and branches (*c*). Next stood we with our torches (*b*), then the musicians (*a*) in a long rank. Last of all, the rest of the virgins (*d*) stood in another long rank. Whence the virgins came, or whether they dwelt in the castle, or whether they were brought in by night, I know not: for all their faces were covered with delicate

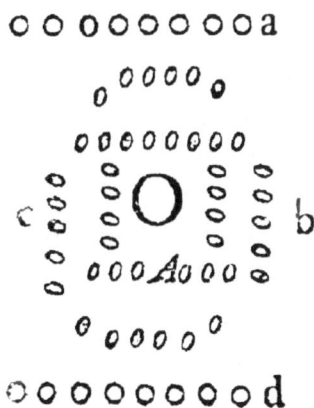

white linen so that I could not know any of them.

Hereupon the Virgin opened the casket, in which there was a round thing wrapped up in a piece of green double-taffeta. This she laid in the uppermost kettle and then covered it with the lid, which was full of holes and had besides a rim. On this she poured in some of the water which we had the day before prepared, whence the fountain began immediately to run through four small pipes to drive into the little kettle. Beneath the undermost kettle there were many sharp points upon which the virgins hung their lamps that so the heat might come to the kettle and make the water seethe. As the water was beginning to simmer, by many little holes in the kettle it fell in upon the bodies, and was so hot that it dissolved them all and turned them into liquor.[2] What the abovementioned round wrapped-up thing was my companions knew not, but I understood that it was the Moor's head, from which the water conceived so great heat.[3] Round about the great kettle, there were again many holes in which they stuck their branches. Whether this was done of necessity or only for ceremony, I know not. However, these branches were continually besprinkled by the fountain, whence it afterwards dropped something of a deep yellow into the kettle.

The fountain still constantly ran of itself for near two hours; but the longer it ran, the fainter it was. Meanwhile, the musicians went their way and we walked up and down in the room; and, truly, the room was so made

2 The *solutio* of alchemy from the maxim "*solve and coalgula*," dissolve and coagulate.

3 A repetition/permutation of the *nigredo*.

that we had opportunity enough to pass away our time. There was, for images, paintings, clockworks, organs, springing fountains, and the like, nothing forgotten. At last it was near the time that the fountain ceased and would run no longer, upon which the Virgin commanded a round golden globe to be brought.

At the bottom of the fountain there was a tap by which she let out all the matter that was dissolved by those hot drops (whereof certain quarts were then very red)[4] into the globe. The rest of the water which remained above in the kettle was poured out. And so this fountain (which was now become much lighter) was again carried forth. Now, whether it was opened abroad or whether anything of the bodies that was further useful yet remained, I dare not certainly say. But this I know: that the water that was emptied into the globe was much heavier than six (or even more of us) were well able to bear, albeit for its bulk it should have seemed not too heavy for one man.

Now this globe being with much ado gotten out of doors, we again sat alone. But I, perceiving a trampling overhead, had an eye to my ladder. Here one might take notice of the strange opinions my companions had concerning this fountain. For they, not imagining but that the bodies lay in the garden of the castle, knew not what to make of this kind of working, but I thanked God that I awaked in so opportune a time and saw that which helped me the better in all the Virgin's business.

After one quarter of an hour the cover above was

4 The *rubedo*, or red stage in alchemy, which presages the resurrection stage. See Lyndy Abraham, *Dictionary of Alchemical Imagery*, 174–75.

again lifted off and we commanded to come up, which was done as before with wings, ladders, and ropes. It did not a little vex me that, whereas the virgins could go up another way, we were fain to take so much toil; yet I could well judge there must be some special reason in it, and that we must leave somewhat for the old man to do as well. For even those with the wings had no advantage by them but when they were to mount through the hole.

Being gotten up thither and the hole shut again, I saw the globe hanging by a strong chain in the middle of the room. In this room was nothing else but plain, clear windows, and between each pair of windows there was a door which was covered with nothing but a great polished looking-glass. These windows and looking-glasses were so optically opposed one to another that although the sun (which now shined exceeding bright) beat only upon one door, yet (after the windows towards the sun were opened and the doors before the looking-glasses drawn aside) in all quarters of the room there was nothing but suns, which by artificial refractions beat upon the whole golden globe hanging in the midst. And for as much as the globe (besides that brightness) was polished, it gave such a lustre that none of us could open our eyes but were forced to look out of the windows till the globe was well-heated and brought to the desired effect. Here I may well avow that in these mirrors I have seen the most wonderful spectacle that ever Nature brought to light: for there were suns in all places and the globe in the middle shined yet brighter, so that, but for one twinkling of an eye, we could no more endure it than the sun itself.

At length, the Virgin commanded to shut up the looking-glasses again and to make fast the windows, and so to let the globe cool again a little. This was done about seven of the clock. We thought this good, since we might now have leisure a little to refresh ourselves with a breakfast. This treatment was right philosophical, and we had no need to be afraid of intemperance; yet we had no want. Indeed, the hope of the future joy (with which the Virgin continually comforted us) made us so jocund that we regarded not any pains or inconvenience. And this I can truly say, too, concerning my companions of high quality: that their minds never ran after their kitchen or table, but that their pleasure was only to attend upon this adventurous physick and hence to contemplate the Creator's wisdom and omnipotency.

After we had taken our refection, we again settled ourselves to work, for the globe was sufficiently cooled. With toil and labour we were to lift off the chain and set it upon the floor. The dispute was how to get the globe asunder: for we were commanded to divide the same in the middle. The conclusion was that a sharp pointed diamond would best do it. When we had thus opened the globe, there was nothing of redness more to be seen, but a lovely great snow-white egg.[5] It most mightily rejoiced us that this was so well brought to pass. For the Virgin was in perpetual care lest the shell might still be too tender.

We stood round about this egg as jocund as if we ourselves had laid it. But the Virgin made it presently be carried forth, and departed herself from us again, and

5 The "egg" is the vessel in which the transmutation of the *materia* into the Philosopher's Stone takes place.

(as always) locked the door to. What she did abroad with the egg, or whether it were some way privately handled, I know not, neither do I believe it. Yet, we were again to pause together for one quarter of an hour, till the third hole were opened, and we by means of our instruments were come upon the fourth stone or floor.

In this room we found a great copper kettle filled with yellow sand which was warmed with a gentle fire. Afterwards, the egg was raked up in it, that it might therein come to perfect maturity. This kettle was exactly square, and upon one side stood these two verses writ in great letters:

O. BLI. TO. BIT. MI. LI.
KANT. I. VOLT. BIT. TO. GOLT.[6]

On the second side were these three words:

SANITAS. NIX. HASTA.[7]

The third had no more but this one word:
F. I. A. T.[8]

---

6 This inscription has given commentators more than a little trouble. Both Montgomery (2:447) and Adam Maclean follow Alfons Rosenberg's modern German edition of the *CW* (1957, 164–65) which argues it may stand for OBLI(gatio). BIT(umen). LI(queficatumque). KANT or CANT(ione). I(gnique). VOLT(us). BIT(uminous). TO(llitur). GOLT., which would translate as "Prescription: Take pulverized and liquefied fusible bitumen; through music and fire the form of the bitumen is elevated to gold." Maclean admits this a speculative solution of the puzzle, but it is certainly compelling. See Maclean's commentary to *The Chemical Wedding of Christian Rosenkreutz*, trans. Joscelyn Godwin (Grand Rapids, MI: Phanes Press, 1991), 142.

7 "Health. Snow. Spear."

But on the hinder most part stood an entire inscription running thus:

QVOD.
Ignis: Aer: Aqua: Terra:
SANCTIS REGUM ET REGINARUM NOSTR:
Cineribus.
Eripere non potuerunt.
Fidelis Chymicorum Turba
IN HANC URNAM
Contulit.
Ao.[9]

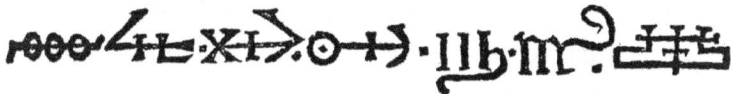

8 Both "Let there be" (*Fiat*) and also *Fluidus, Ignis, Aether, Terra* (Water, Fire, Air, Earth). Montgomery (*Cross and Crucible*, 2:449) interprets the initials as standing for *Forma, Igne, Arteque, Transformatur*, which isn't half bad, but, given what follows (see note 9), the elements seem to be more in keeping with the mood here.

9 "What Fire, Air, Water, Earth were not able to tear from the holy ashes of our Kings and Queen a crowd of faithful chymists has given to this urn. A.D. 1459." Kienast deciphers the code as follows:

1000 = +1000
< = −100 (subtract because before the D)
I = −1 (subtract because before the X)
L = +50
X = +10
D = +500
_____
1459

Montgomery (*Cross and Crucible*, 2:451) entertains the thought that the symbols may represent the signs of the zodiac, reading them, left to right, as Aquarius; Capricorn and Leo; Pisces and Sagittarius; Cancer; Gemini and Scorpio; Virgo and Aries; Taurus over Libra. Could be.

Now whether the sand or egg were hereby meant, I leave to the learned to dispute; yet do I my part and omit nothing undeclared.

Our egg being now ready was taken out. It needed no cracking, however, for the bird that was in it soon freed himself and shewed himself very jocund—yet he looked very bloody and unshapen. We first set him upon the warm sand, for the Virgin commanded that before we gave him anything to eat, we should be sure to make him fast, otherwise he would give us all work enough. This being done, food was brought him, which surely was nothing else than the blood of the beheaded, diluted again with prepared water, by which the bird grew so fast under our eyes that we well saw why the Virgin gave us such warning of him. He bit and scratched so devilishly about him that could he have had his will upon any of us he would soon have dispatched him.

He was wholly black and wild, wherefore other meat was brought him, which was perhaps the blood of another of the Royal Persons. At this, all his black feathers moulted again, and instead of them there grew but snow-white feathers. He was somewhat tamer, too, and suffered himself to be more tractable; nevertheless, we did not yet trust him.

At the third feeding, his feathers began to be so curiously coloured, that in all my life I never saw the like colours for beauty.[10] He was also exceeding tame, and behaved himself so friendly with us that (the Virgin consenting) we released him from his captivity.

---

10 In alchemy this stage is known as the *cauda pavonis*, "peacock's tail." It occurs immediately before the *nigredo* stage.

"'Tis now reason," began our Virgin, "since, by your diligence and our old man's consent, the bird has attained both his life and the highest perfection, that he be also joyfully consecrated by us." Herewith she commanded to bring in dinner and bade that we should again refresh ourselves, since the most troublesome part of our work was now over and it was fit we should begin to enjoy our passed labours. We began to make ourselves merry together, howbeit we had still all our mourning clothes on, which seemed somewhat reproachful to our mirth. The Virgin then was perpetually inquisitive, perhaps to find to which of us her future purpose might prove serviceable. But her discourse was for the most part about melting; and it pleased her well when anyone seemed expert in such compendious manuals as do peculiarly commend an artist. This dinner lasted not above three quarters of an hour, which we for the most part spent with our bird, whom we were fain constantly to feed with his meat, but he still continued much at the same growth.

After dinner we were not long suffered to digest our meat, and after that the Virgin together with the bird was departed from us. The fifth room was set open to us, whither we got to after the former manner and tendered our service. In this room a bath was prepared for our bird, which was now coloured with a fine white powder that it had the appearance of pure milk.[11] It was

---

11. The bath (*balenum*) is, like baptism, the water of purification prior to the regeneration of the *materia*. Milk (*lac virginis*, or virgin's milk) is the solution in which the materia in washed prior to the *coniunctio oppositorum* of Sol and Luna, King and Queen. As Michael Maier notes

at first cool when the bird was set into it: he was mighty well pleased with it, drinking of it and pleasantly sporting in it. But, after it began to heat by reason of the lamps that were placed under it, we had enough to do to keep him in the bath. We therefore clapped a cover on the kettle and suffered him to thrust his head out through a hole till he had in this sort lost all his feathers in this bath and was as smooth as a newborn child. Yet the heat did him no further harm, at which I much marveled. In this bath the feathers were quite consumed, and the bath was thereby tinged blue.

At length we gave the bird air, and he of himself sprung out of the kettle, and was so glitteringly smooth that it was a pleasure to behold it. But, because he was still somewhat wild, we were fain to put a collar with a chain about his neck and so led him up and down the room. In the meantime a strong fire was made under the kettle and the bath sodden away till it all came to a blue stone, which we took out. Having first pounded it, we were afterwards fain to grind it on a stone, and finally with this colour to paint the bird's whole skin over. At this he looked much more strangely, for he was all blue except the head, which remained white.

Herewith our work on this story was performed, and (after the Virgin with her blue bird was departed from us) we were called up through the hole to the sixth story, which was done. There we were mightily trou-

---

in *Atalanata Fugiens*, "The Stone should be fed, just as a child, with the milk of a Virgin" (Michael Maier, *Atalanta Fugiens* [1617], ed. H.M.E. de Jong [Leiden: E.J. Brill, 1969], 98). Correspondences to the Virgin Mary nursing the infant Christ are not hard to draw from such a notion.

bled: for in the midst a little altar was placed, every way like that in the King's hall above described. Upon the altar stood the six aforementioned particulars, and he himself (that is, the bird) made the seventh. First of all, the little fountain was set before him, out of which he drunk a good draught. Afterwards he pecked upon the white serpent until she bled mightily. This blood we were to receive into a golden cup and pour down the bird's throat. He was mighty averse from it. Then we dipped the serpent's head in the fountain, upon which she again revived and crept into her death's-head: I saw her no more for a long time after.

Meanwhile, the sphere turned constantly on until it made the desired conjunction. Immediately the watch struck one, upon which there was another conjunction. Then the watch struck two. Finally, whilst we were observing the third conjunction and the same was indicated by the watch, the poor bird of himself submissively laid down his neck upon the book and willingly suffered his head (by one of us thereto chosen by lot) to be smitten off. Howbeit, he yielded not one drop of blood till he was opened on the breast—and then the blood spun out so fresh and clear as if it had been a fountain of rubies.

His death went to the heart of us, and yet we might well judge that a naked bird would stand us in little stead. So we let it rest and removed the little altar away and assisted the Virgin to burn the body to ashes (together with the little tablet hanging by) with fire kindled at the little taper and afterwards to cleanse the same several times and to lay them in a box of cypress wood.

Here I cannot conceal what a trick I and three more

were served. After we had thus diligently taken up the ashes, the Virgin began to speak thus:

"My lords, we are here in the sixth room and have only one more before us, in which our trouble will be at an end, and then we shall return home again to our castle to awaken our most gracious lords and ladies. As it is, I heartily wish that all of you, as you are here together, had behaved yourselves in such sort that I might have given you commendations to our most renowned King and Queen and you might have obtained a suitable reward: yet, contrary to my desire, I have found amongst you these four (herewith she pointed at me and three more) lazy and sluggish labourators. Nevertheless, according to my good-will to all and everyone, am I not willing to deliver them up to condign punishment. However, that such negligence may not remain wholly unpunished, I am purposed thus concerning them: that they shall only be excluded from the future seventh and most glorious action of all the rest, and so, too, they shall incur no further blame from their Royal Majesties."

In what a case we now were at this speech, I leave others to consider: for the Virgin so well knew how to keep her countenance that the water soon ran over our baskets and we esteemed ourselves the most unhappy of all men. After this the Virgin by one of her maids (whereof there were many always at hand) caused the musicians to be fetched who were with cornets to blow us out of doors with such scorn and derision that they themselves could hardly sound for laughing. But it did particularly mightily afflict us that the Virgin so vehemently laughed at our weeping, anger, and impatience, and that there might well perhaps be some amongst our companions who were glad of this our misfortune. But it proved otherwise.

As soon as we were come out at the door, the musicians bid us be of good cheer and follow them up the winding-stairs. They led us up to the seventh floor, under the roof, where we found the old man, whom we had not hitherto seen, standing upon a little round furnace. He received us friendly and heartily congratulated us that we were hereto chosen by the Virgin. But after he understood the fright we had conceived, his belly was ready to burst with laughing, that we had taken such good fortune so heinously. "Hence," said he, "my dear sons, learn that man never knoweth how well God intendeth him."

During this discourse the Virgin, along with her little box, came running in. After she had sufficiently laughed at us, she emptied her ashes out into another vessel and filled hers again with other matter, saying she must now go cast a mist before the other artists' eyes and that we in the meantime should obey the old lord in whatsoever he commanded us and not remit our former diligence. Herewith she departed from us into the seventh room, whither she called our companions. What she first did with them there I cannot tell, for they were not only most earnestly forbidden to speak of it, but we, too (by reason of our business) durst not peep on them through the ceiling. But this was our work: we were to moisten the ashes with our fore-prepared water till they became altogether like a very thin dough. After this we set the matter over the fire till it was well heated, then cast it thus hot as it was into two little forms or moulds, and so let it cool a little.

At this point, we had leisure to look awhile upon our

companions through certain crevices made in the floor. They were now very busy at a furnace, and each was himself fain to blow up the fire with a pipe. They stood thus blowing about it, as if they were ready to lose their breath, although they imagined they were herein wondrously preferred before us. And this blowing lasted so long till our old man roused us to our work again, so I cannot say what was done afterwards.

Having opened our little forms, there appeared two beautiful, bright, and almost transparent little images, the like to which man's eye never saw: a male and a female, each of them only four inches long.[12] What most mightily surprised me was that they were not hard but as limber and fleshy as other human bodies, yet had they no life. Indeed, I do most assuredly believe that the Lady Venus's image was also made after some such way. These angelically fair babes we first laid upon two little satin cushionettes and beheld them a good while till we were almost besotted upon so exquisite an object. The old lord warned us to forbear and continually to instill the blood of the bird (which had been received into a lit-

---

12 The homunculus represents the birth of the Philosophical Child which still must be nurtured in order to be brought to complete perfection, an idea J.W. von Goethe explores in the second part of *Faust*. Paracelsus writes of the homunculus at length in *De Natura Rerum* and, among other things, describes it as "a miracle and marvel of God, an arcanum above arcana, and deserves to be kept secret until the last times, when there shall be nothing hidden, but all things shall be made manifest." See *The Hermetic and Alchemical Writings of Paracelsus the Great*, trans. and ed. Arthur Edward Waite (London: J. Elliott & Co., 1894), 1:124–25. Montgomery wisely notes that the homunculi of the *CW*, unlike those of Paracelsus, are not hermaphroditic (*Cross and Crucible*, 2:459). For more on this idea, see my essay in this volume.

tle golden cup) drop after drop into the mouths of the little images, from whence they apparently to the eye increased. Whereas they were before very small, they were now (according to proportion) much more beautiful: so that worthily all limners[13] ought to have been here and have been ashamed of their art in respect of these productions of Nature.

They began to grow so big that we lifted them from the little cushionettes and were fain to lay them upon a long table which was covered with white velvet. The old man also commanded us to cover them over up to the breast with a piece of fine white double-taffeta: this, because of their unspeakable beauty, almost went against us. But that I may be brief: before we had in this manner quite spent the blood, they were already in their perfect full growth. They had gold-yellow curled hair and the above-mentioned figure of Venus was nothing to them. But there was not yet any natural warmth or sensibility in them: they were dead figures, yet of a lively and natural colour. And since care was to be taken that they grew not too great, the old man would not permit anything more to be given them, but quite covered their faces with the silk and caused the table to be stuck round about with torches.

Here I must warn the reader that he imagine not these lights to have been of necessity; for the old man's intent hereby was only that we should not observe when the soul entered into them, as, indeed, we should not have taken notice of it if I had not twice before seen the flames. However, I permitted the other three to remain

13 Painters of miniatures.

in their belief; neither did the old man know that I had seen anything more.

Hereupon he bade us sit down on a bench over against the table. Presently the Virgin came in with the music and all furniture and carried two curious white garments, the like to which I had never seen in the castle; neither can I describe them, for I thought no other but that they were pure crystal, but they were gentle and not transparent. For that I cannot speak of them. These she laid down upon a table and, after she had disposed her virgins upon a bench round about, she and the old man began many legerdemain tricks about the table, which was done only to blind us. This (as I told you) was managed under the roof, which was wonderfully formed: for on the inside it was arched into seven hemispheres, of which the middlemost was somewhat the highest, and it had at top a little round hole, which was nevertheless shut and observed by none else.

After many ceremonies, stepped in six virgins, each of which bare a large trumpet which was circled about with a green glittering and burning material like a wreath. One of these the old man took and, after he had removed some of the lights at top and uncovered their faces, he placed one of the trumpets upon the mouth of one of the bodies in such manner that the upper and wider part of it was directed just against the aforementioned hole. Here my companions always looked upon the images. But I had other thoughts: for, as soon as the foliage or wreath about the shank of the trumpet was kindled, I saw the hole at top open and a bright stream of fire shooting down the tube and passing into the body, whereupon the hole was again covered and the trumpet removed. With this device my companions were deluded that they imagined that life came into the image by means of the fire of the foliage: for as soon as he received the soul he twinkled with his eyes, howbeit he scarce stirred. The second time, he placed another tube upon its mouth and kindled it again and the soul was let down through the tube. This was repeated upon each of them three times, after which all the lights were extinguished and carried away. The velvet carpets of the table were cast together over them and immediately a child's travelling bed[14] was unlocked and made ready, into which thus wrapped up they were borne. And so, after the carpets were taken off them, they were neatly laid by each other and with the curtains drawn before them slept a good while.

Now was it also time for the Virgin to see how our other artists behaved themselves. They were well pleased because (as the Virgin afterwards informed me) they were to work in gold, which is, indeed, a piece also of this art, but not the most principal, most necessary, and best.[15] They had, also, a part of these ashes, so that they imagined no other but that the whole bird was provided for the sake of gold, and that life must thereby be restored to the deceased. During this, we sat very still, attending when our married couple would awake. And thus about half an hour was spent.

At that moment, the wanton Cupid presented himself

---

14 A child's portable bed or cradle. In early modern German, *Reyßbet-tlein*.

15 Gold-making, contrary to the popular misconception of alchemy, was not the primary research interest of those engaged in the Work.

again, and, after he had saluted us all, flew to them behind the curtain, tormenting them so long till they awaked. This happened to them with very great amazement, for they imagined no other but that they had hitherto slept from the very hour in which they were beheaded. Cupid, after he had awaked them and renewed their acquaintance one with another, stepped aside a little and permitted them both somewhat better to recruit themselves. Meanwhile, he played his tricks with us and at length he would needs have the music fetched to be somewhat the merrier. Not long after this, the Virgin herself came and, after she had most humbly saluted the young King and Queen (who found themselves somewhat faint) and kissed their hands, she brought them the two aforementioned curious garments. These they put on, and so stepped forth. There were already prepared two very curious chairs, wherein they placed themselves, and so were by us with most profound reverence congratulated. For this the King in his own person most graciously returned his thanks, and again reassured us of all grace. It was already about five of the clock, wherefore they could make no longer stay. Then, as soon as ever the chiefest of their furniture could be laden, we were to attend the young Royal Persons down the winding-stairs through all doors and watches unto the ship, in which they embarked themselves together with certain virgins and Cupid, and sailed so mighty swift that we soon lost sight of them. They were met (as I was informed) by certain stately ships and thus in four-hours' time they had made many leagues out at sea.

After five of the clock, the musicians were charged to

carry all things back again to the ships and to make themselves ready for the voyage. Because this was somewhat long a doing, the old lord commanded forth a party of his concealed soldiers (who had hitherto been planted in the wall so that we had taken no notice of any of them). From this I observed that the Tower was well provided against opposition. The soldiers made quick work with our stuff, so that no more remained further to be done but to go to supper.

The table being completely furnished, the Virgin brought us again to our companions—though we were to carry ourselves as if we had truly been in a lamentable condition and forbear laughing. But they were always smiling one upon another, howbeit some of them sympathized with us. At this supper the old lord was with us, too, and he was a most sharp inspector over us: for none could propound anything so discreetly but that he knew how either to confute it or to amend it or at least to give some good document upon it. I learned most by this lord, and it were very good that each one would apply himself to him and take notice of his procedure: for then things would not so often—and so untowardly —miscarry.

After we had taken our nocturnal refection, the old Lord led us into his closets of rarities which were here and there dispersed amongst the bulwarks. There we saw such wonderful productions of Nature and other things which man's wit in imitation of Nature had invented that we needed a year more sufficiently to survey them. Thus we spent a good part of the night by candlelight. At last, because we were more inclined to sleep than see many rarities, we were lodged in rooms in the wall where we had not only costly good beds, but also besides extraordinary handsome chambers, which made us the more wonder why we were the day before forced to undergo so many hardships. In this chamber I had good rest; and being for the most part without care (and weary with continual labour) the gentle rushing of the sea helped me to a sound and sweet sleep: for I continued in one dream from eleven of the clock till eight in the morning.

The Seventh Day

AFTER eight of the clock I awaked and quickly made myself ready, being desirous to return again into the Tower, but the dark passages in the wall were so many and various that I wandered a good while before I could find the way out. The same happened to the rest, too, till at last we all met again in the nethermost vault where habits entirely yellow were given us together with our Golden Fleeces. At that time the Virgin declared to us that we were Knights of the Golden Stone, of which we were before ignorant. After we had thus made our selves ready and taken our breakfast, the old man presented each of us with a medal of gold. On the one side stood these words:

AR. NAT. MI.[1]

On the other these:

TEM. NA. F.[2]

He exhorted us, moreover, that we should enterprise nothing beyond and against this token of remembrance. Herewith we went forth to the sea, where our ships lay so richly equipped that it was not well possible but that such brave things must first have been brought thither. The ships were twelve in number: six of ours and six of

---

1 *Ars naturae ministra*, "Art the Priestess of Nature."
2 *Temporis natura filia*, "Nature the Daughter of Time."

the old lord's, who caused his ships to be freighted with well-appointed soldiers. But he betook himself, to us, into our ship, where we all were together. In the first ship the musicians seated themselves, of which the old lord had also a great number. They sailed before us to shorten the time. Our flags were the twelve celestial signs, and we sat in Libra.[3] Besides other things, our ship had also a noble and curious clock which shewed us all the minutes. The sea was so calm that it was a singular pleasure to sail. But that which surpassed all the rest was the old man's discourse: he so well knew how to pass away our time with wonderful histories that I could have been content to sail with him all my life long. In the meantime, the ships passed on amain,[4] for before we had sailed two hours the mariner told us that he already saw the whole lake almost covered with ships, by which we could conjecture they were come out to meet us, which also proved true. And as soon as we were gotten out of the sea into the lake by the river, there presently stood in to us five-hundred ships, one of which sparkled with pure gold and precious stones and in which sat the King and Queen together with other lords, ladies, and virgins of high birth.

As soon as they were well in ken of us, the cannons were discharged on both sides, and there was such a din of trumpets, shawms, and kettle drums that all the ships upon the sea capered again. Finally, as soon as we came

3 That is, in the center, Libra being the balances and the seventh of the twelve constellations—and the only constellation depicted as a non-living thing, all the rest being one variety or another of mythical animal or human.

4 "At full speed."

near, they brought about our ships together, and so made a stand. Immediately, the old Atlas stepped forth on the King's behalf making a short (but handsome) oration. He welcomed us and demanded whether the royal presents were in readiness. The rest of my companions were in a huge amazement whence this King should arise from the dead, for they imagined no other but that they must again awaken him. We suffered them to continue in their wonderment and carried ourselves as if it seemed strange to us, too. After Atlas's oration, out steps our old man making somewhat a larger reply wherein he wished the King and Queen all happiness and increase, after which he delivered up a curious small casket. But what was in it, I know not, only that it was committed to Cupid, who hovered between them both, to keep.

After the oration was finished, they again let off a joyful volley of shot, and so we sailed on a good time together, till at length we arrived at another shore. This was near the first gate at which I first entered. At this place there attended a great multitude of the King's family together with some hundreds of horses. As soon as we were come to shore and disembarked, the King and Queen presented their hands to all of us, one with another with singular kindness, and so we were to get up on horseback.

(*Here I desire to have the reader friendly entreated not to interpret the following narration to any vainglory or pride of mine, but to credit me thus far: that if there had not been a special necessity in it, I could very well have utterly concealed this honour which was shewed me.*)

We were all one after another distributed amongst the lords. But our old lord and I (most unworthy) were to ride with the King, each of us bearing a snow-white ensign with a red cross. I, indeed, was made use of because of my age, for we both had long grey beards and hair. I had besides fastened my tokens round about my hat, of which the young King soon took notice and demanded if I were he who could at the gate redeem these tokens. I answered in most humble manner, "Yea." But he laughed on me, saying there henceforth needed no ceremony: I was *his* father! Then he asked me with what I had redeemed them. "With water and salt," I replied, whereupon he wondered who had made me so wise. At this, I grew somewhat more confident and recounted unto him how it had happened to me with my bread, the dove, and the raven, and he was pleased with it. He said expressly that it must needs be that God had herein vouchsafed me a singular happiness.

Herewith we came to the first gate where the porter with the blue clothes waited and who bore in his hand a supplication. As soon as he spied me with the King, he delivered me the supplication, most humbly beseeching me to mention his ingenuity towards me before the King. First I demanded of the King what the condition of this porter was. He friendly answered me that he was a very famous and rare astrologer, always in high regard with the lord his father. But having on a time committed a fault against Venus, and beheld her in her bed of rest, this punishment was therefore imposed upon him: that he should so long wait at the first gate till someone should release him from thence. I replied, "May he then be released?" "Yes," said the King, "if anyone can be found that hath as highly transgressed as himself, he must stand in his stead and the other shall be free."

This word went to my heart, for my conscience convinced me that I was the offender, yet I held my peace and herewith delivered the supplication. As soon as he had read it, he was mightily terrified, so that the Queen, who (with our virgins and the other queen besides, of whom I made mention at the hanging of the weights) was riding just behind us observed it and asked him what this letter might signify. But he had no mind that he should take notice of it, but, putting up the paper, began to discourse of other matters. Thus in about three hours' time we came quite to the castle, where we alighted and waited upon the King into his aforementioned hall.

Immediately the King called for the old Atlas to come to him in a little closet and shewed him the writing. Atlas made no long tarrying, but rode out again to the porter to take better cognizance of the matter. After this the young king with his spouse and other lords, ladies, and virgins sat down. Then began our Virgin highly to commend the diligence we had used and the pains and labour we had undergone, requesting we might be royally rewarded and that she henceforward might be permitted to enjoy the benefit of her commission. Then the old lord stood up and attested that all that the Virgin had spoken was true, and that it was but equity that we should on both parts be contented. Hereupon we were to step out a little. It was then concluded that each man should make some possible wish and accordingly obtain it: for it was not to be doubted but that those of understanding would also make the best wish. And so we were to consider of it till after supper.

Meanwhile, the King and Queen for recreation's sake

began to fall to play together. It looked not unlike chess, only it had other laws: for it was the virtues and vices, one against another, where it might ingeniously be observed with what plots the vices lay in wait for the virtues, and how to reencounter them again. This was so properly and artificially performed that it were to be wished that we had the like game, too. During the game, in came Atlas again and made his report in private. Yet I blushed all over: for my conscience gave me no rest.

After this, the King presented me the supplication to read. The contents whereof were much to this purpose: first he wished the King prosperity and increase and that his seed might be spread abroad far and wide. Afterwards he remonstrated that the time was now accomplished wherein according to the royal promise he ought to be released. This was because Venus had already been uncovered by one of his guests: for his observations could not lie to him. If His Majesty would please to make a strict and diligent enquiry, he would find that she had been uncovered and, in case this should not prove so to be, he would be content to remain before the gate all days of his life. Then he sued in the most humble manner that upon peril of body and life he might be permitted to be present at this night's supper, as he was in good hopes to spy out the very offender and obtain his desired freedom. This was expressly and handsomely indicted, by which I could well perceive his ingenuity; but it was too sharp for me, and I could well have endured never to have seen it. At this point, I was casting in my mind whether he might perchance be helped through my wish, so I asked the King whether he might not be released some other way.

"No," replied the King, "because there is a special consideration in the business. However, for this night we may well gratify him in his desire." He then sent one forth to fetch him in.

Meanwhile, the tables were prepared in a spacious room in which we had never been before: it was so complete and in such manner contrived that it is not possible for me to begin to describe it. Into this room we were conducted with singular pomp and ceremony. Cupid was not at this time present, for (as I was informed) the disgrace which had happened to his mother had somewhat angered him. In brief, my offence and the supplication which was delivered were an occasion of much sadness, for the King was in perplexity how to make inquisition amongst his guests: and the more because even they who were yet ignorant of the matter would come to the knowledge of it. So he caused the porter himself, who was already come, to make his strict survey and shewed himself as pleasant as he was able.

At length, they began again to be merry and to bespeak one another with all sorts of recreative and profitable discourses. How the treatment and other ceremonies were then performed, it is not necessary to declare—since it is neither the reader's concern nor serviceable to my design. But all exceeded more in art and human invention than that we were overcharged with drinking. And this was the last and noblest meal at which I was present. After the banquet, the tables were suddenly taken away and certain curious chairs placed round about in circle. In these we together with the King and Queen, both their old men, the ladies, and virgins were to sit. After which a very handsome page opened the above mentioned glorious little book when Atlas immediately placing himself in the midst began to bespeak us to the ensuing purpose: that his Royal Majesty had not yet committed to oblivion the service we had done him and how carefully we had attended our duty; and, therefore, by way of retribution, he had elected all and each of us Knights of the Golden Stone. It was, therefore, further necessary not only once again to oblige ourselves towards His Royal Majesty, but to vow upon the following articles. Thus his Royal Majesty would likewise know how to behave himself towards his liege people. At this, he caused the page to read over the articles, which were these:

I. You, my lords the knights, shall swear that you shall at no time ascribe your order either unto any devil or spirit, but only to God your Creator and his handmaid Nature.

II. That you will abominate all whoredom, incontinency, and uncleaness, and not defile your order with such vices.

III. That you through your talents will be ready to assist all that are worthy and have need of them.

IV. That you desire not to employ this honour to worldly pride and high authority.

V. That you shall not be willing to live longer than God will have you.

At this last article we could not choose but laugh sufficiently, and it may well have been placed after the rest only for a conceit. Now, being to vow to them all by the King's scepter, we were afterwards with the usual ceremonies installed knights, and amongst other privileges set over ignorance, poverty, and sickness, to handle them at our pleasure. And this was afterwards ratified in a little chapel (whither we were conducted in all procession) and thanks returned to God for it. There I also at that time, to the honour of God, hung up my Golden Fleece and hat and left them there for an eternal memorial; and because everyone was there to write his name, I writ thus:

Summa Scientia nihil Scire.
Fr. *CHRISTIANUS ROSENCREUTZ*
Eques aurei Lapidis.
Anno. 1459.[5]

Others writ otherwise and truly, each as seemed him good. Then we were again brought into the hall, where, being sat down, we were admonished quickly to bethink ourselves what everyone would wish. The King and his party, however, retired into a little closet, there to give audience to our wishes. Each man was called in severally, so that I cannot speak of any man's proper wish. I thought nothing could be more praiseworthy than in

---

5 "The sum of knowledge is to know nothing. Fr. Christian Rosenkreutz. Knight of the Golden Stone. In the year 1459." Note the similarity to the oracle of Delphi's assessment of Socrates: that he was the wisest of all men because he claimed to know nothing.

honour of my order to demonstrate some laudable vir-
tue and found that none at present could be more
famous and cost me more trouble than gratitude.
Therefore, not regarding that I might well have wished
something more dear and agreeable to myself, I vanquished myself and concluded, even with my own peril,
to free my benefactor, the porter.

Being now called in, I was first of all demanded
whether, having read the supplication, I had observed
or suspected nothing concerning the offender. At once,
I began undauntedly to relate how all the business had
passed: how through ignorance I fell into that mistake,
and so offered myself to undergo all that I had thereby
demerited. The King and the rest of the lords wondered
mightily at so unhoped-for a confession and so wished
me to step aside a little.

As soon as I was called for in again, Atlas declared to
me that, although it were grievous to the King's Majesty that I whom he loved above others was fallen into
such a mischance, yet, because it was not possible for
him to transgress his ancient usages, he knew not how
else to absolve me but that the other must be at liberty
and I placed in his stead. Yet he would hope that some
other would soon be apprehended, that so I might be
able to go home again. However, no release was to be
hoped for till the marriage feast of his future son.

This sentence had near cost me my life, and I first
hated myself and my twattling tongue that I could not
hold my peace. Yet at last I took courage, and, because I
considered there was no remedy, I related how this porter had bestowed a token on me and commended me to
the other, by whose assistance I stood upon the scale

and so was made partaker of all the honour and joy already received. Therefore, now it was but equal that I should shew myself grateful to my benefactor. Because the same could no way else be done, I returned thanks for the sentence and was willing gladly to sustain some inconvenience for his sake, who had been helpful to me in coming to so high place. But if by my wish anything might be effected, I wished myself at home again: that so he by me and I by my wish might be at liberty.

Answer was made me that the wishing stretched not so far. However, I might well wish him free. Yet it was very pleasing to his Royal Majesty that I had behaved myself so generously herein, but he was afraid I might still be ignorant into what a miserable condition I had plunged myself through this my curiosity. Hereupon the good man was pronounced free and I, with a sad heart, was fain to step aside.

After me, the rest were called for, too. They came jocundly out again, which was still more to my smart: for I imagined no other but that I must finish my life under the gate. I had also many pensive thoughts running up and down in my head concerning what I should yet undertake and wherewith to spend the time. At length, I considered that I was now old and, according to the course of nature, had few years more to live and that this anguish and melancholy life would easily dispatch me and my doorkeeping would be at an end; and that by a most happy sleep I might quickly bring myself into the grave. I had sundry of these thoughts. Sometimes it vexed me that I had seen such gallant things and must be robbed of them. Sometimes it rejoiced me that before my end I had been accepted to all joy and

should not be forced shamefully to depart. Thus this
was the last and worst shock that I sustained.

During these my cogitations the rest were ready,
wherefore after they had received a good night from the
King and lords each one was conducted into his lodging. But I, most wretched man, had nobody to show me
the way, and yet must moreover suffer myself to be tormented. Also, that I might be certain of my future func-
tion, I was fain to put on the ring which the other had
before worn. Finally, the King exhorted me that since
this was now the last time I was like to see him in this
manner I should nevertheless behave myself according
to my place and not against the order. At this, he took
me in his arms and kissed me: all which I so understood
as if in the morning I must sit at my gate. After they had
all a while spoken friendly to me and at last presented
their hands, committing me to the divine protection, I
was by both the old men (the lord of the Tower and
Atlas) conducted into a glorious lodging in which stood
three beds, and each of us lay in one of them. There we
yet spent almost two, &c.

*Here are wanting about two leaves in quarto, in which he
(the author hereof), imagining he must in the morning be
doorkeeper, returned home.*[6]

FINIS.

6 Some commentators take this claim as fact, but it seems another of
Andreae's jokes and may be a parody of the end of Plato's *Critias* which
likewise breaks off in the middle of Plato's description of the destruction
of Atlantis. Andreae's ending of the tale has been the object of (sometimes
bizarre, indeed) speculation ever since it was published.

Marriage and *The Chymical Wedding*: A Consideration

*"Zehre mit Geisterglut meinen Leib, daß ich luftig mit dir
inniger mich mische und dann ewig die Brautnacht währt."*
~ *Novalis, Hymnen an die Nacht*[1]

*"Deinde seipsa complectuntur & coeunt, & lux moderna ab eis
gignitur, cui nulla lux similis est per totum mundum."*
~ *Daniel Mylius, Philosophia reformata*[2]

HE word "marriage," as recent history has shown,
can no longer be assumed to signify universal cultural archetypes of "husband" and "wife." Indeed,
our postmodern, post-religious, and indeed post-biological
cultural norms have become increasingly—sometimes mili-
tantly—hostile to what John Milbank describes as "the
essential significance of biblical engendered typology" and
"the biblical and theological significance of sexual differ-
ence."[3] To even mention this biblical schema in most con-

1. "Tear my body with spirit fire, so I can mix with you more
inwardly, airily, and then the wedding night will last forever." Novalis,
Hymns to the Night, trans. Dick Higgins (New York: McPherson & Company, 1984), 13.
2. "Then they embrace and unite and the new light is born of them,
which is like no other light through all the world." Ioannis Danielis Mylis,
Philosophia reformatat... (Francofurtii, 1622), 244.
3. John Milbank, "Sophiology and Theurgy: The New Theological
Horizon" in *Encounter between Eastern Orthodoxy and Radical Orthodoxy*,
ed. Adrian Pabst and Christoph Schneider (Farnham, UK: Ashgate, 2009),
45–85, at 83.

temporary academic and social milieux, in fact, is to invite outrage and ridicule.

But that doesn't mean one shouldn't.

The Chymical Wedding of Christian Rosenkreutz and its highly idiosyncratic (even for alchemy) symbolic cosmos, though its tableau offers an array of bizarre and intriguing imaginative images, nevertheless locates the holistically simple idea of marriage at the center of its philosophical, scientific, and theological commitments. From the invitation that arrives on the first day to the accomplishment of the work on the sixth (following Genesis, the alchemists rest on the seventh day), the notion of marriage—as permeated by the erotic, as paradigm, as *coincidentia oppositorum*—haunts every page of the text. *The Chymical Wedding*'s telos, that is, intends toward an eschatological marriage evocative of the denouement of the book of Revelation when John beholds "the holy city, new Jerusalem, coming down out of the heaven from God, prepared as a bride adorned for her husband" (22:2). Yet to read *The Chymical Wedding* (let alone Revelation) and what it says about marriage as a quaint if nevertheless irrelevant artifact of a bygone era is to entirely—and tragically—miss the significance of the ideas it entertains as they can be applied to our own cultural moment.

Eros

One thing that is quite obvious in surveying the alchemical process depicted in *The Chymical Wedding* is its utter lack of *eros*. On the sixth day, for example, the alchemists (having already been vetted in a process mirroring the alchemical stages) engage themselves in a rather mundane (despite its fantastic nature) and laborious routine of preparing the

materia: a sequence of solutions, coagulations, precipita-
tions, burnings, illuminations, deaths, and sublimations. As
Christian complains, "we were fain to be mere drudges till
we had achieved all that was necessary for the restoring of
the beheaded bodies."[4] The *narrative* outside of the alchemical work proper, however, is charged with the erotic.

First of all, and perhaps too obviously, the existence of the
concept of marriage implies the presence of the erotic. In
the early modern period no less than at other times, marriage was understood as a procreative institution concerned,
among many other things, with fertility and the raising of
children as exemplified by Genesis's injunction "Be fruitful
and multiply" (1:28). But despite what some theorists have
asserted,[5] this was not simply a business transaction with
birthed children as the currency of a very real human capi-
tal. Rather, marriage was understood as a divine ordinance,
an ontological structure of the cosmos. In short: it's how
things work. And *eros*, as Plato was so aware[6] and Christian
mysticism has upheld, infuses all that is.

While classical philosophical speculations about *eros*
tended to diminish the importance of gendered typology
(without entirely discounting it), the Genesis account of
creation attends more phenomenologically, one might even
say more scientifically, to the ontological structures of being
in this world: "Let us create man in our image, after our
likeness. . . . in the divine image he created him; male and
female he created them" (1:26, 27). Indeed, István Cselényi

4. Page 115.
5. See, for example, Stephanie Coontz, *Marriage, a History: How Love
Conquered Marriage* (New York: Viking, 2005).
6. Particularly in the *Symposium*.

wonders, as did Alexis van der Mensbrugghe before him, whether the "us" of Genesis 1:26 implies the feminine Sophia, the Wisdom of God, as God's partner in such creation—which is certainly a more consistent reading of gendered biblical typology (and supported by Proverbs 8 among other scriptural witnesses).[7] Indeed, Margaret Barker's recent scholarly excavations of First Temple Judaism suggest that the originary form of Jewish worship included reverence for Wisdom before she was expelled from the Temple and all but expunged from scripture following the reforms of Josiah.[8] In the light of Barker's discoveries, perhaps the intuitions of Cselényi and Mensbrugghe (as well as my own) are not all that unfounded.[9]

Eros has always been regarded in Christian tradition as a force that not only permeates the cosmos but that drives human persons to seek God. This is apparent in Augustine, for example, and is fully illustrated in the Song of Songs. As Benedict XVI has written:

> From the standpoint of creation, *eros* directs man toward marriage, to a bond which is unique and definitive; thus, and only thus, does it fulfill its deepest purpose.... Marriage based on exclusive and definitive love becomes the icon of the relationship between God and his people and

7. István Cselényi, *The Maternal Face of God? Explorations in Catholic Sophiology*, trans. Bulcsú Hoppal, Attila Tárnok, Bence Biró (Kettering, OH: Angelico Press, 2017), 167–68. Alexis van der Mensbrugghe, *From Dyad to Triad: A Plea against Duality and an Essay toward the Synthesis of Orthodoxy* (London: The Faith Press, 1935), 26.

8. Much of Barker's work focuses on this aspect of the First Temple; see in particular her *The Mother of the Lord, Volume I: The Lady in the Temple* (London: Bloomsbury, 2012).

9. See my *The Submerged Reality: Sophiology and the Turn to a Poetic Metaphysics* (Kettering, OH: Angelico Press, 2015).

vice versa. God's way of loving becomes the measure of human love. This close connection between *eros* and marriage in the Bible has practically no equivalent in extra-biblical literature.[10]

Or, in the words of Mechthild of Magdeburg:

> I must go from all things to God,
> Who is my Father by nature,
> My Brother by his humanity,
> My Bridegroom by love,
> And I his bride from all eternity.[11]

As it is in Mechthild's writing, *eros* is the content of *The Chymical Wedding*. Indeed, in the first paragraph Christian finds his meditation disrupted by a "twitching" behind him and finds "a fair and glorious lady whose garments were all sky-colour and curiously (like Heaven) bespangled with golden stars."[12] The gender of the figure is not inconsequential, and the operative term here is "twitching."[13] She hands Christian the invitation at the bottom of which stand the words *Sponsus* and *Sponsa*, bridegroom and bride (echoes of Christ and the Church as Bridegroom and Bride are not coincidental). As in several other points of the narrative, a very real physiobiological effect takes place in our protagonist, as Christian reports: "As soon as I had read this letter, I was presently like to have fainted away, all my hair stood on

10. *Encyclical Letter of the Supreme Pontiff Benedict XVI: Deus Caritas Est*, 11.

11. Mechthild of Magdeburg, *The Flowing Light of the Godhead*, trans. Frank Tobin, The Classics of Western Spirituality (New York: Paulist Press, 1998), 61.

12. Page 12.

13. The German word here translated as "twitching" (*mahlen*) also means "grind," adding a further alchemical connotation to the narrative.

end, and a cold sweat trickled down my whole body." That is to say, the alchemical work simultaneously provokes both objective (on the *materia*) as well as subjective (on the alchemist) reactions, the latter preceding the former as a psychosomatic activity: a kind of phenomenological disclosure, a quantum phenomenon.

And then there is this business of virgins.

Throughout the tale, a number of virgins cajole, entice, and otherwise stimulate the alchemists (and more particularly Christian Rosenkreutz himself) in their progress toward achieving the chymical wedding. Their primary device is *eros*, and first among them is the Virgin, who directs the proceedings and becomes Christian's patron and guide. Christian describes her on The Second Day,

> At last the two aforementioned pages with bright torches entered the hall, lighting in a most beautiful Virgin, drawn upon a gloriously gilded triumphant self-moving throne. It seemed to me she was the very same who before on the way kindled and put out the lights, and that these her attendants were the very same whom she formerly placed at the trees. She was not now as before in sky-colour, but arrayed in a snow-white glittering robe which sparkled of pure gold and cast such a lustre that we durst not steadily behold it.[14]

The resonances between Christian's Virgin and the iconography of the Woman Clothed with the Sun of Revelation 12 and the Virgin Mary are not hard to detect, and this model clearly informs the figure who appears to Christian with the invitation on The First Day. Catholic interpretations of the Woman of Revelation 12 uniformly associate her with the

14. Page 98.

Virgin Mary, though Protestant exegesis, going back at least to the time of the Geneva Bible, interprets this figure as the Church, safeguarding real anxieties about the role of Mary in salvation, even though the Church appears in Revelation 21 as the New Jerusalem. Though Andreae was a Lutheran, and eventually a pastor, and despite Protestantism's eschewal of Marian devotion, the divine feminine found a way to permeate his imagination and its productions. His Virgin is not a cipher for the Church as separate from the Virgin Mary, but of a mediatrix synonymous with her. For Vladimir Solovyov this mediatrix (Sophia) likewise participates in the onto-reality of the Virgin Mary, the Church, and Christ himself.[15] As it does with Edmund Spenser in *The Faerie Queen* and the *Hymne of Heavenly Beautie*, and with John Milton in his repeated invocations of the Muse in *Paradise Lost*, the divine feminine in *The Chymical Wedding* infiltrates Andreae's Protestant psyche as an *incognito* Virgin Mary. As with the Virgin Mary in salvation history, Christian's Virgin moves the alchemical work (as well as the narrative) toward its conclusion. Without her nothing can be accomplished.

Throughout the tale, the virgins (and the Virgin) also flirt with Christian and the other alchemists, as for instance in the bed game of The Fourth Day. The joke is definitely on the alchemists:

> The Virgin instantly made the proposal that we should mix ourselves together in a ring, and that she beginning to count from herself, the seventh, was to be content with the following seventh, whether it were a Virgin or man. For our parts, we were not aware of any craft, and there-

15. Vladimir Solovyov, *Russia and the Universal Church*, trans. Herbert Rees (London: Geoffrey Bles, 1948), 169.

fore permitted it so to be. But when we thought we had very well mingled ourselves, the virgins nevertheless were so subtle that each one knew her station beforehand. The Virgin began to reckon, the seventh next her was again a virgin, the third seventh a virgin likewise, and this happened so long till (to our amazement) all the virgins came forth and none of us was hit. Thus we poor pitiful wretches remained standing alone, and were moreover forced to suffer ourselves to be jeered, too, and confess we were very handsomely cozened.[16]

Eros, the narrative argues, moves the Work, as it indeed moves everything. As Guillaume Apollinaire has it, it is "*L'amour qui emplit ainsi que la lumière / Tout le solide espace entre les étoiles et les planets.*"[17] Love fills like light all solid space between the stars and planets. The song chanted by the sea nymphs on The Fifth Day attests to this:

> *Who gets herein the victory? 'Tis Love.*
> *Can Love by search obtainéd be? By Love.*
> *How may a man good works perform? Through Love.*
> *Who into one can two transform? 'Tis Love.*[18]

The last line is particularly germane to the work of the chymical wedding.

Eros also appears in the story in a more obvious way: as Cupid. Cupid makes his first entrance on The Fourth Day as the King, Queen, virgins, alchemists, and other attendants gather around a mysterious fountain and an equally mysterious altar. As Christian describes it:

16. Page 89.
17. Guillaume Apollinaire, "Poème lu au Mariage d'Andre Salmon," lines 40–41.
18. Page 112.

Here can I not pass in silence how the little Cupid flew to and again there, but for the most part he hovered and played the wanton about the great crown. Sometimes he seated himself in between the two lovers, somewhat smiling upon them with his bow. Nay, sometimes he made as if he would shoot one of us. In brief, this knave was so full of his waggery that he would not spare even the little birds, which in multitudes flew up and down the room, but tormented them all he could. The virgins also had their pastimes with him: but whensoever they could catch him, it was not so easy a matter for him to get away from them again. Thus this little knave made all the sport and mirth.[19]

Cupid likewise agitates the flame of the candle upon the altar as well as the serpent which coils itself around a skull, "unless it happened that Cupid twitched a little at her, for then she slipped in so suddenly that we all could not choose but marvel at it." (Note the reappearance of the word "twitched.") Cupid similarly twitches the King himself, though he saves his most merciless antagonizing for Christian, who complains that Cupid "could not leave us (and me especially) untormented."[20] And nowhere is Cupid's involvement more crucial to the narrative and its eros than in the vignette concerning his mother, Venus.

At the beginning of The Fifth Day, Christian accompanies his page to the tomb of Venus, a site which, as Christian hears, is "the King's treasury."[21] The sepulcher, we are told,

was triangular and had in the middle of it a kettle of polished copper; the rest was of pure gold and precious

19. Page 86.
20. Page 87.
21. Page 104.

> stones. In the kettle stood an angel who held in his arms
> an unknown tree from which fruits continually dropped
> into the kettle; and as oft as the fruit fell into the kettle, it
> turned into water and ran out from thence into three
> small golden kettles standing by. This little altar was sup-
> ported by these three animals: an Eagle, an Ox, and a
> Lion, which stood on an exceeding costly base.

This sepulcher includes some important features. First of all,
it is triangular (which may suggest the Trinity). The kettle is
made of copper, which, as just about anyone of the early
modern period would have known, was the metal corre-
spondent to the planet Venus. Venus (Aphrodite in Greek)
is, of course, the goddess of love, just as Venus in Ptolemaic
astrology is the planet of love. As such, Venus is also the
planet (and tutelary spirit) of the wedding, another irrup-
tion of the divine feminine in this allegedly Protestant
mythos.

Marriage, of course, is also in Catholic teaching numbered as one of the seven sacraments. Medieval and early
modern natural philosophers, alchemists, and their ilk were
fond of drawing tables of correspondences: connecting the
sacraments to the planets and metals (among many other
things) would have been a matter of course for them. In his
system, the nineteenth-century Catholic occultist Éliphas
Lévi (Alphonse Louis Constant), for example, draws these
connections:

> Baptism, which consecrates the element of water, corre-
> sponds to the moon; ascetic penance is under the auspices
> of Samael, the angel of Mars; confirmation, which imparts
> the spirit of understanding and communicates to the true
> believer the gift of tongues, is under the auspices of
> Raphael, the angel of Mercury; the Eucharist substitutes

the sacramental realization of God made man for the empire of Jupiter; marriage is consecrated by the angel Anael, the purifying genius of Venus; extreme unction is the safeguard of the sick about to fall under the scythe of Saturn; and orders, consecrating the priesthood of light, is marked more especially by the characters of the sun.[22]

Organons of correspondences like Lévi's were quite commonplace in the Renaissance and even influenced the art of painting. In discoursing on the symbolic importance of the color green, for example, the sixteenth-century Italian poet, playwright, and art critic Raffaello Borghini relates that

among virtues it demonstrates Fortitude, Venus among planets, lead among the metals, youth up to thirty-five years among the ages of man, Thursday among days, spring among the seasons, April, dark green, and May, bright green, among the months, and Marriage among the sacraments.[23]

This is a poetic metaphysics that recognizes cosmological as well as liturgical dimensions in all of the created order. The heavens for some can still declare the glory of God, but such a cosmological assumption is now a rarity. Andreae would have worked out of a similar, if not identical, schema to those of Lévi and Borghini (nuance is the prerogative of the intellectual after all). Alchemical texts are rife with symbolic and planetary correspondences and *The Chymical Wedding* reifies the traditional alchemical correspondences of Venus to marriage and copper.

22. Éliphas Lévi, *Transcendental Magic: Its Dogma and Ritual*, trans. Arthur Edward Waite (London: George Redway, 1896), 236–37.
23. Raffaello Borghini, *Il Riposo*, trans. and ed. Lloyd H. Ellis, Jr., Lorenzo Da Ponte Italian Library (Toronto: University of Toronto Press, 2007), 153.

The three animals supporting the kettle—the Eagle, Bull, and Lion (Scorpio, Taurus, and Leo)—of course have long-standing correspondences to the Holy Living Creatures of Ezekiel's vision of the chariot and their permutations in Revelation as well as to the writers of the gospels of John, Luke, and Mark, respectively—but where is the fourth figure, the man or angel (Aquarius)? Does Andreae suggest that Christian represents the fourth? The text does not say, though it is tempting to surmise that the tripartite structure of the tomb suggests a work as yet incomplete (Venus is, after all, entombed) and only to be completed at the realization of the chymical wedding itself through the catalyzing effect of human participation. Threeness, that is, desires fourness. Indeed, we might hazard to propose that the Holy Trinity was incomplete without the acquiescence of the Virgin to make the incarnation a reality, thereby bringing God into full physical presence among his creatures, an intuition Sergei Bulgakov developed at length.[24] C.G. Jung's enthusiasm for the promulgation of the dogma of the *Assumptio Mariae* in 1950, in fact, was deeply informed by such a schema and what he saw as its psychological necessity for Western culture:

> For a long time there had been a psychological need for this, as is evident in the medieval pictures of the Assumption and Coronation of the Virgin; it was also responsible for elevating her to a position as Mediatrix, corresponding to Christ's position as mediator. . . . The recent promulga-

24. See in particular his *The Bride of the Lamb*, trans. Boris Jakim (Grand Rapids, MI/Edinburgh, UK: William B. Eerdmans Publishing Company, 2002) and *Sophia, the Wisdom of God: An Outline of Sophiology*, trans. Patrick Thompson, O. Fielding Clarke, and Xenia Braikevitic, revised (Hudson, NY: Lindisfarne Press, 1993).

tion of the dogma of the Assumption emphasizes the taking up not only of the soul but of the body of Mary into the Trinity.[25]

The notion of a mediatrix, as we have seen, also surfaces in *The Chymical Wedding*.

In the sepulcher, Christian receives an unanticipated gift: he beholds Venus unveiled:

> Herewith I espied a rich bed readymade and hung about with curious curtains, one of which [the page] drew, where I saw the Lady Venus stark naked (for he heaved up the coverlets, too) lying there in such beauty and in a fashion so surprising that I was almost beside myself. Neither do I yet know whether it was a piece thus carved or a human corpse that lay dead there, for she was altogether immoveable—and yet I durst not touch her. She was again covered and the curtain drawn before her, yet she was still (as it were) in my eye.

During the Florentine Renaissance, Ficino wrote of Venus as "the power that moves the visible world, infusing the transcendent order into the corporal,"[26] a palimpsest of which persists in *The Chymical Wedding*.[27] The vision of Venus presages Christian's achievement of the chymical wedding, even though he receives a wound (from her son Cupid) for his transgression: no one who touches the *mysterion* comes

25. C.G. Jung, *Mysterium Coniunctionis: An Inquiry into the Separation and Synthesis of Psychic Opposites in Alchemy*, 2nd ed., trans. R.F.C. Hull, Bollingen Series XX (Princeton: Princeton University Press, 1970), 186.

26. From *De amore*, 6.8; cited and translated by Edgar Wind in his *Pagan Mysteries in the Renaissance* (New Haven: Tale University Press, 1958), 119–20.

27. Ficino, indeed, is Ioan Couliano's starting point in *Eros and Magic in the Renaissance*.

away from the encounter unscathed. But can an eternal goddess in fact die? Can she really be dead? Indeed, is the goddess of love and spirit of marriage not even now entombed? Does she await new Christian Rosenkreutzes to undertake the adventure of restoring her? In Andreae's time the metaphor of the veiled and hidden goddess was simultaneously scientific and theological.[28] Today it remains both of these things. But it is also political.

Eros and Thanatos

Death, as Freud was certainly not the first to note, is never far from considerations of *eros*; and *The Chymical Wedding of Christian Rosenkreutz*, as also the entire alchemical *corpus*, illustrates *par excellence* the imaginal synergy of *eros* and *thanatos* as perhaps no other literature does. Deaths occur in almost all alchemical literature of the medieval and early modern periods, and the idea of the death and resurrection of Christ informs this notion to a significant degree. As the alchemical tract *The Glory of the World* has it: "The body of Christ had to be separated from its soul in order that it might receive the same power and glory. But now, Christ having been dead, and His soul having afterwards been reunited with His body, they are henceforth inseparably conjoined into one subtle essence."[29]

The alchemical project, it is my contention, began with

28. See, for example, Pierre Hadot, *The Veil of Isis: An Essay on the History of the Idea of Nature*, trans. Michael Chase (Cambridge: The Belknap Press of Harvard University Press, 2006).

29. *The Glory of the World* in *The Hermetic Museum, Restored and Enlarged...*, ed. Arthur Edward Waite, 2 vol. (1893; reprt., York Beach, ME: Samuel Weiser, Inc., 1990), 1:169.

an investigation into the regeneration of matter, of man, and of creation. As such, it could be realized fully in no other culture than a Christian one. It was a science of resurrection, and alchemists invested themselves in discovering the glorified bodies of the *materia* upon which they experimented, an ethos evident in the research into palingenesis undertaken by, among many others, Paracelsus in the sixteenth century and Kenelm Digby in the seventeenth.[30] Alchemy, like so many academic disciplines, eventually degenerated into more utilitarian applications;[31] but in its essence it was a truly Christian science.

Nevertheless, the idea of physical as well as spiritual regeneration was also taken up in the Russian religious philosophy and theology of the late-nineteenth and early-twentieth centuries. Vladimir Solovyov, for one, argued that: "Our regeneration is indissolubly bound up with the regeneration of the universe and with the transfiguration of its forms of space and time."[32] And Sergei Bulgakov considered

30. See the chapter entitled "Love's Alchemist: Palingenesis and the Unconscious Metalepsis of Sir Kenelm Digby" in my *Literature and the Encounter with God in Post-Reformation England* (Farnham, UK: Ashgate, 2014).

31. René Guénon proposes that our current assumption that astrology and alchemy have "evolved" into modern astronomy and chemistry is fallacious. "If the latter sciences do in a certain sense come from the former," he writes, "it is not by 'evolution' or 'progress'—as is claimed—but on the contrary by degeneration." Considering the spiritual and philosophical poverty of reductive scientific materialism, maybe he has a point. See his *The Crisis of the Modern World*, trans. Marco Pallis, Arthur Osborne, and Richard C. Nicholson (Hillsdale, NY: Sophia Perennis, 2004), 48.

32. Vladimir Solovyov, *The Meaning of Love*, trans. Jane Marshall, rev. and ed. Thomas R. Beyer, Jr. (Hudson, NY: Lindisfarne Press, 1985), 104.

the Crucifixion of Christ not only an event that regenerated man, but likewise redeemed nature; and, as a result of the Deed of Golgotha, for Bulgakov the earth itself has become the Holy Grail, for it is the vessel that has received the blood of the Master:

> The whole world is the Holy Grail, for it has received into itself and contains Christ's precious blood and water. The whole world is the chalice of Christ's blood and water; the whole world partook of them in communion at the hour of Christ's death. And the whole world hides the blood and water within itself. A drop of Christ's blood dripped upon Adam's head redeemed Adam, but also all the blood and water of Christ that flowed forth into the world sanctified the world. The blood and water made the world a place of the presence of Christ's power, prepared the world for its future transfiguration, for the meeting with Christ come in glory.... The world has become Christ, for it is the holy chalice, the Holy Grail.[33]

The death and regeneration depicted in alchemical treatises traces this profoundly Christian template.

In alchemy, the death in question is sometimes that of Mercurius, sometimes that of a king and queen, sun and moon, or various animals. In *The Chymical Wedding* we find a veritable bloodbath: three royal pairs of kings and queens are slaughtered and entombed while the team of alchemists is commissioned with combining them and bringing them back to life. Christian encounters them at the banquet on The Fourth Day:

33. Sergius Bulgakov, *The Holy Grail and the Eucharist*, trans. Boris Jakim (Hudson, NY: Lindisfarne Books, 1997), 43–44.

This room was square on the front, five times broader than it was long; but towards the west it had a great arch like a porch, wherein stood in circle three glorious royal thrones, the middlemost was somewhat higher than the rest. Now in each throne sat two persons. In the first sat a very ancient king with a gray beard, yet his consort was extraordinary fair and young. In the third throne sat a black king of middle age and by him a dainty old matron, not crowned but covered with a veil. But in the middle sat the two young persons, who, though they had likewise wreaths of laurel upon their heads, yet over them hung a large and costly crown.[34]

At the conclusion of the banquet "a very coal-black, tall man who bare in his hand a sharp axe" beheads all six, and their bodies and blood are preserved in six coffins especially prepared for them.[35] Then the executioner himself is beheaded.

On The Sixth Day, the alchemists hatch a bird from an egg made from the remains of the kings and queens—but, after a sequence of form and behavior changes allegorical of the alchemical stages, it too is beheaded and subsequently burned. From the ashes of the bird the alchemists fashion the bodies of two homunculi—a tiny king and queen— which they feed with the bird's blood (which they had previously collected) in order to make them grow. The homunculi eventually reach human proportion and receive life, not from the exertions of the alchemists in burning wreaths at this point (as they are led to believe), but from the surreptitious introduction of fire into their bodies by the subterfuge of the virgins (which only Christian notices): "With this

34. Page 85.
35. Page 100.

device my companions were deluded that they imagined that life came into the image by means of the fire of the foliage: for as soon as he received the soul he twinkled with his eyes, howbeit he scarce stirred."[36]

Death, then, proves an essential component of the chymical wedding. It is essential because the Crucifixion is essential to both the Resurrection and the regeneration of mankind. This brings us back to *eros* and its *telos*.

Coniunctio oppositorum

Charles Williams argues that sexual intercourse between a man and a woman "is, or at least is capable of being, in a remote but real sense, a symbol of the Crucifixion. There is no other human experience, except Death, which so enters into the life of the body; there is no other human experience which so binds the body to another human being."[37] As Pope Francis has instructed, "the sacrament of marriage flows from the incarnation and the paschal mystery."[38] Marriage, moreover, as the Book of Revelation and even the Greek mysteries witness, is a *telos*[39] but without its elevation to mysticism it inhabits a realm that is neither mysterious nor sacred and becomes a fraud, a sham, a carcass: something in need of regeneration. "Marriage as a sacrament,

36. Page 134.

37. Charles Williams, *Outlines of Romantic Theology with which is reprinted "Religion and Love in Dante: The Theology of Romantic Love,"* ed. Alice Mary Hadfield (Berkeley, CA: The Apocryphile Press, 2005), 24.

38. Pope Francis, *Post-Synodal Apostolic Exhortation: Amoris Lætitia*, 74.

39. Jane Harrison, *Prolegomena to the Study of Greek Religion* (Cambridge University Press, 1908), 534.

mystical marriage," writes Nicolas Berdyaev, "is by its very meaning eternal and indissoluble. This is an absolute truth. But most marriages have no mystical meaning and have nothing to do with eternity. The Christian consciousness must recognize this."[40] This is a hard saying.

In the alchemical literature, the *coniunctio oppositorum* (conjunction of opposites) emblematizes an important paradigm of human flourishing: it is only by uniting opposites that the miracle can occur and the work be accomplished. As *The Golden Tract* has it:

> Know that the secret of the work consists in male and female, i.e., an active and a passive principle. In lead is found the male, in orpiment the female. The male rejoices when the female is brought to it, and the female receives from the male a tinging seed, and is coloured thereby.[41]

This *telos*, indeed, reaches beyond the grave and realizes its promise in the glorified body, which the alchemists were so bold as to assay with their *materia* this side of the Parousia. It is no surprise then that the marriages of alchemical practitioners Kenelm Digby and Thomas Vaughan figure so strongly in their own work. Digby, whose wife Venetia predeceased him by over thirty years, considers her glorification with scientific candor: "I can not place the resurrection of our bodies among miracles, but do reckon it the last worke and periode of nature; to the comprehension of which, examples and reason may carry us a great way."[42]

40. Nicolas Berdyaev, *The Destiny of Man*, trans. Natalie Duddington (New York: Harper Torchbooks/The Cloister Library, 1960), 234.

41. In *Hermetic Museum*, 1:14.

42. Vittorio Gabrieli, ed., "A New Digby Letter-Book: 'In Praise of Venetia,'" *National Library of Wales Journal* 9, no. 2 (1955): 455.

Vaughan's wife Rebecca (whom he referred to as "Thalia" in much of his writing)[43] served not only as his life partner, but also as his partner in alchemical experimentation; and she continued to inspire him and his work through his dream-life following her untimely death at the age of twenty-seven in 1658. As Donald R. Dickson describes it, for Thomas, even after her death Rebecca served as "tutelary spirit through the medium of his dreams, as spiritual lover who teaches him the sublime mysteries of eternal versus earthly love . . . and as idealized muse."[44] The idea of a "chymical wedding" certainly had other than materialistic applications for Digby and Vaughan.[45]

The mystical understanding of marriage, albeit now compromised by legalistic and absolutely un-erotic determinations conditioned by a ghastly parody of the chymical wedding joining neoliberalism, socialism, and capitalism, persists in some quarters of contemporary culture not under obligation to religious or political ideology. In Lindsay Clarke's novel *The Chymical Wedding* (inspired by the life and work of Maryann Atwood),[46] for example, the nar-

43. After the muse of comedy and idyllic poetry. Her name means "the flourishing."

44. Donald R. Dickson, Introduction to *Thomas and Rebecca Vaughan's Aqua Vitæ: Non Vitis* (British Library MS, Sloane 1741), ed. and trans. Donald R. Dickson (Tempe, AZ: Arizona Center for Medieval and Renaissance Studies, 2001), xxxi.

45. The notion also persists in the legend of the alchemical undertakings of Nicolas and Perenelle Flamel.

46. Atwood (1817–1910) was the author of one of the most curious works on alchemy written since the seventeenth century: *A Suggestive Inquiry into the Hermetic Mystery, with a Dissertation on the more Celebrated Alchemical Philosophers, being an Attempt towards the Recovery of the Ancient Experiment of Nature* (Belfast: William Tait, 1918).

rator Alex Darken explains the importance of such a gendered typology: "many alchemists had worked with a female
assistant—a *soror mystica*—for the Art required that both
aspects of human nature, the male and female, the solar and
lunar, be reconciled in harmonious union if the chymical
wedding was to be celebrated."[47] Likewise, in the climax
(note the apt metaphor) of Wim Wenders's film *Der Himmel
über Berlin* (known to English-speaking audiences as *Wings
of Desire*), the trapeze artist Marion instructs her beloved,
the newly incarnated in the flesh angel Damiel, regarding
the significance of such a union:

> You and I are now time itself. Not only the whole city—the
> whole world is taking part in our decision. We're more
> than just the two of us now. We embody something. We're
> sitting in Das Platz des Volkes. And the whole place is full
> of people with the same dream as ours. We are defining the
> game for everyone. I'm ready. Now it's your turn. You hold
> the game in your hand. It's now... or never. You need me.
> You will need me. There is no greater story than ours, that
> of man and woman. It will be a story of giants... invisi-
> ble... transposable... a story of new ancestors. Look... my
> eyes. They are the image of necessity, of the future of
> everyone in the place. Last night... I dreamed of a
> stranger... of my man. Only with him could I be alone,
> open up to him, wholly open, wholly for him... welcome
> him wholly into me. Surround him with the labyrinth of
> shared happiness. I know... it's you.

Indeed, the union of the mortal Marion and the incarnated
angel Damiel, marriage of matter and spirit, is nothing if

---

47. Lindsay Clarke, *The Chymical Wedding* (New York: Alfred A.
Knopf, 1989), 162.

not an image from the pages of alchemical tracts of the seventeenth century, only translated into a postmodern idiom filtered through the language of Rilke. And I have nothing but admiration for Wenders when we hear the applause (ostensibly for Nick Cave and the Bad Seeds) at precisely the moment when Marion and Damiel kiss.

Jung, in searching for a model for psychic well-being, looked to the integration of male and female (*animus* and *anima*) as the goal of psychology. He called this "a higher union . . . an indispensable prerequisite for wholeness,"[48] and his long fascination with alchemy certainly bears witness to this insight. Of this union—which is a true communion—he writes:

> They therefore represent a supreme pair of opposites, not hopelessly divided by logical contradiction but, because of the mutual attraction between them, giving promise of union and actually making it possible. The *coniunctio oppositorum* engaged the speculations of the alchemists in the form of the "Chymical Wedding," and those of the cabalists in the form of Tifereth and Malchuth or God and the Shekinah, not to speak of the marriage of the Lamb.[49]

Adding to Jung's examples we might point to the creative participation of Sophia with God depicted in the biblical literature: unfortunately, most of the Fathers and the greater part of the theologians to follow have preferred to keep her in the exile of personification—perhaps the source of the psychic unrest that pervades western civilization at our own cultural moment. As Margaret Barker has argued, it was not

48. C.G. Jung, *Aion: Researches into the Phenomenology of the Self,* trans. R.F.C. Hull, 2nd ed., Bollingen Series XX (Princeton: Princeton University Press, 1959), 32.

49. Ibid., 268.

always thus.[50] But, as we all know only too well, gendered typology has not had an easy go of it of late.

Alchemical literature often includes hermaphroditic images, which some might wish to hold up as more fitting emblems of our times than the chymical wedding and the *coniunctio oppositorum*. But this would be a mistake. The hermaphrodite, the *Rebis* or *Lapis Philosophorum* in other imaginative constellations, represents, as Jung rightly asserts, not only the achieved union of opposites but "a symbol of the self . . . a union of conscious (masculine) and unconscious (feminine)."[51] There are no hermaphrodites in Andreae's tale. The hermaphrodite is an interior reality, an interior integration. Sans integration, it is pathology, a pathology projected onto and manifesting in the tableau of culture. It has nowhere else to go.

Every marriage, therefore, needs to be a chymical marriage, a mystical marriage. For it is the case that, as Berdyaev argues, "the eternity and indissolubility of marriage is an ontological and not a social truth."[52] Otherwise, we have nothing but pathology: a caricature of marriage and not a metaphysical truth. Only a marriage between a man and a woman can embody this. A marriage that does not realize the union of a man and a woman, the *coniunctio oppositorum*, cannot properly be construed a marriage despite the presence of its political or ideological justification, for the political and the ideological are simply pathology writ large— and this can be true as well of heterosexual arrangements that do not manifest their union to this degree. Indeed, the

50. Margaret Barker, *The Mother of the Lord, Volume I: The Lady in the Temple* (London: Bloomsbury, 2012).

51. C.G. Jung, *Aion*, 268.

52. Nicolas Berdyaev, *The Destiny of Man*, 235.

existence of bad heterosexual marriages in no way delegiti-
mizes the ontological reality of what marriage is. This too is
a hard saying.

Marriage, that is, is an ontological and metaphysical reality; in the language of the Schoolmen, a universal. Nominal-
ism, the tutelary philosophy of our age, cannot alter this
reality, though it tries to avoid its truth by dismissing it as
"culturally constructed" or as simply a reflection of a society's norms. Disturbingly, such malaise indicates all too well
that we are party to an "implicit teleology of the gradual
exclusion of all otherness."[53] Laws and customs may change,
dictionaries may change: ontology and metaphysics do not.
As Paul Evdokimov argued, "Without a metaphysic, without
a return to the beginning, the human being can never be
grasped; there will always remain a residue that is irreducible to history and pure phenomenology. Only then will we
be able to deal with the archetypal constitution of man and
the distinction between the charismatic conditions of man
and woman."[54] To understand marriage—between the
Bridegroom and the Bride, between God and Sophia,
between man and woman—as the archetypal constitution
underpinning all biological, somatic, psychic, pneumatic,
and supernatural existence is imperative to human flourishing. For the world is, indeed, a wedding;[55] and each wedding has the potential to become the world. We must return

53. Slavoj Žižek, *Violence: Six Sideways Reflections* (New York: Pica-
dor, 2008), 32.

54. Paul Evdokimov, *Woman and the Salvation of the World: A Christian Anthropology on the Charisms of Women*, trans Anthony P. Gythiel
(Crestwood, NY: St. Vladimir's Seminary Press, 1983), 16.

55. See A.M. Allchin, *The World is a Wedding: Explorations in Christian Spirituality* (New York: Oxford University Press, 1978).

to the beginning that is always already happening, the kairotic moment that acknowledges "the birth of the simple light / In the first, spinning place" when "it was all / Shining" when "it was Adam and maiden."[56]

Epilogue

The poets, then, may be the most successful psychologists, the most successful alchemists to whom we can turn; and Andreae's *Chymical Wedding* is clearly a work of poetry. Indeed, among other poets, Andreae here, Dante in the *Commedia*, and Novalis in *Hymnen an die Nacht* whisper to us of the only authentic *cura animarum*. Likewise does the Song of Songs speak to this: "Let him kiss me with the kisses of his mouth."[57] John Donne also knew the secret:

> Wee then, who are this new soule, know,
> Of what we are compos'd, and made,
> For, th'Atomies of which we grow,
> Are soules, whom no change can invade.[58]

The secret, of course, is no secret, but, more properly, a *mysterion*. Marriage, as with all of the sacraments, is something into which we are initiated, immersed, but is not something we are able to fully comprehend. And it is also a vessel of grace. The *coniunctio oppositorum* emblematized in marriage possesses not only psychological significance but also illuminates ontological, metaphysical, and biological realities.

56. Dylan Thomas, "Fern Hill," lines 33–34, 29–30.
57. 1:1.
58. John Donne, "The Extasie," from *The Complete of John Donne*, ed. John Shawcross (Garden City, NY: Anchor Books, 1967), lines 41–44.

Hence the primal significance of marriage between a man and a woman. It is not good that either one should be alone. For the *coniunctio* is the doorway to psychic, ontological, and metaphysical, as well as biological regeneration.

Mais chaque spectateur cherchait en soi l'enfant miraculeux
Siècle ô siècle des nuages.[59]

---

59. Guillaume Apollinaire, "Un Fantôme de Nuées," lines 76–77.

www.ingramcontent.com/pod-product-compliance
Lightning Source LLC
Chambersburg PA
CBHW032059080426
42733CB00006B/343